CW01335699

10 Steps to Happiness

*Helping You Navigate the
Path to Happiness to Live
a More Meaningful Life*

Alice Ford

© **Copyright 2024 - All rights reserved.**

The content contained within this book may not be reproduced, duplicated or transmitted without direct written permission from the author or the publisher.

Under no circumstances will any blame or legal responsibility be held against the publisher, or author, for any damages, reparation, or monetary loss due to the information contained within this book, either directly or indirectly.

Legal Notice:

This book is copyright protected. It is only for personal use. You cannot amend, distribute, sell, use, quote or paraphrase any part, or the content within this book, without the consent of the author or publisher.

Disclaimer Notice:

Please note the information contained within this document is for educational and entertainment purposes only. All effort has been executed to present accurate, up to date, reliable, complete information. No warranties of any kind are declared or implied. Readers acknowledge that the author is not engaged in the rendering of legal, financial, medical or professional advice. The content within this book has been derived from various sources and personal experiences.

By reading this document, the reader agrees that under no circumstances is the author responsible for any losses, direct or indirect, that are incurred as a result of the use of the information contained within this document, including, but not limited to, errors, omissions, or inaccuracies.

Table of Contents

Introduction

Happiness. It can mean different things to different people, and by that fact alone, its meaning is both abstract and completely subjective. Impossible to define in a sentence or two, happiness is more so a feeling or state of being than a definition written on paper. For centuries, different people have developed different meanings for this word. For some, it may be finding peace of mind and inner tranquility.

While for others, it may involve pursuing meaningful relationships, personal growth, or achieving goals that align with their values and passions. Regardless of the unique definition of happiness, this simple word holds immense power over your entire personality and how you look at your life.

Originally, the word *happiness* was taken from the Old English word *hǣpes* or hæpes, which means *good fortune* or *good luck*. This term, in turn, is derived from the Old Norse word *happ*, which also means *good luck* or *chance*. For centuries, different cultures have defined happiness differently. While good fortune and luck are certainly elements of making us happy, it is still up to us as individuals to create the good fortune that we wish to have.

The historian, philosopher, and author of the book *Happiness: A History*, Darrin McMahon defines happiness as follows:

The concept of happiness has been explored and discussed by many philosophers, religious thinkers, and scholars throughout history. In ancient Greek philosophy, happiness was a central topic of inquiry. Aristotle, for instance, considered happiness—*eudaimonia*—as the ultimate goal of human life, encompassing flourishing and the fulfillment of one's potential.

The evolution of *happiness* over time encompasses a broader and deeper understanding of well-being and contentment. It can be described as "a positive emotional and mental state characterized by feelings of joy, satisfaction, fulfillment, and general well-being. It is also often associated with a sense of inner peace, contentment, and a positive outlook on life."

In the modern world, different cultures and belief systems have diverse interpretations of happiness. Some emphasize external factors such as material wealth, success, or social status, while others focus on internal states of mind, contentment, and spiritual well-being.

In today's era, with constant demands, pressures, and uncertainties, finding true happiness can seem like an elusive pursuit. Yet, deep down, we all yearn for a sense of contentment, purpose, and joy in our lives. The quest for happiness is an inherent part of the human experience, and it is a journey that each of us must undertake individually. This pursuit of happiness has led me to write this book and share my strategies for reorganizing your life so that you may find your way to a happier and more fulfilled existence too.

As you undertake this journey it is important to understand, that it is a multi-dimensional and holistic state of being. It encompasses not only our emotional well-being but also our mental, physical, and spiritual health. Plus, it can not only be relied on external factors but should be sought from within our own self.

That's where this book will come in handy for you. From defining who you truly are to defining your goals, broadening your visions, identifying your emotional baggage, learning self-control and the power of self-love, *10 Steps to Happiness* takes a holistic approach, recognizing that true happiness emerges from the harmonious integration of various aspects of our lives.

In each of the 10 chapters, we will delve into essential principles and practices that have stood the test of time, validated by both ancient wisdom and modern science. These steps are not quick fixes or magical solutions but rather a series of intentional actions and mindset shifts that can lead to profound transformation over time.

It is essential to note that happiness is a subjective experience, and its definition may vary from person to person. What brings happiness to one individual may not necessarily bring the same level of happiness to another. Therefore, happiness is deeply personal and influenced by individual values, beliefs, goals, and life circumstances.

The step-by-step approach of this book will help you explore various themes such as self-awareness, gratitude, resilience, mindfulness, authentic connections, purpose, and more. These topics have been carefully selected to provide you with a comprehensive framework that addresses the fundamental elements necessary for building a positive perspective that is essential for happiness and well-being.

By embarking on this transformative exploration, you are investing in yourself and your own well-being. Remember, you deserve happiness, and the pursuit of it is a noble endeavor that can positively impact not only your life but also the lives of those around you.

So, are you ready to take your first step toward happiness? Let us begin this self-care journey toward a healthy mind and body together!

Chapter 1: Defining Who You Are

Happiness starts from within. This is the most common phrase that most of us have heard at least once in life. We are often told that true happiness can only be found by looking within ourselves. But what does that really mean? How do we navigate the depths of our being to uncover the key to our happiness? These are the questions that often leave us confused, searching or yearning for something different, something undefined, something we think will bring us joy. But what is this thing that we are looking for? How do we define it?

Define who you are, and embrace your true authentic self and these questions will all but disappear. My father told me long ago, I could never find love or happiness or long lasting joy until I truly knew myself.

How do we truly know ourselves though?

In today's fast-paced and interconnected world, it is easy to become influenced by societal expectations, external pressures, and the constant need for validation. In the pursuit of happiness, discovering and embracing one's authentic self often goes overlooked. However, in the true sense, this fundamental aspect is the key to happiness.

This self-discovery process is a stepping stone journey toward happiness. Once we know how to do it, it shapes our entire personality. This chapter is dedicated to answering unanswered questions about the happiness journey for you. So, let's dive in together to find out how to do this below!

The Importance of Defining Who You Are

Self-awareness is the basis of a confident personality. Likewise, defining who you are forms the foundation of a fulfilling and purposeful life. Understanding the fact that your identity provides clarity, direction, and a sense of belonging in a world that often feels overwhelming and chaotic is a true blessing in disguise. Most of us remain unaware of this fact. Therefore, we always end up with wrong choices in search of happiness.

Defining who you are empowers you to make informed decisions that align with your values and aspirations. It allows you to establish boundaries and prioritize what truly matters to you, enabling you to navigate life's challenges with authenticity and confidence.

As Nelson Mandela said (2013):

> Education is the great engine of personal development. It is through education that the daughter of a peasant can become a doctor, that the son of a mineworker can become the head of the mine, that a child of farmworkers can become the president of a great nation. It is what we make out of what we have, not what we are given, that separates one person from another.

Knowing who you are fosters self-acceptance and self-love. You can embrace your individuality and build a positive self-image by recognizing your strengths, weaknesses, and unique qualities. This self-awareness cultivates a deep sense of inner peace and contentment.

The famous author Benjamin Franklin, in his autobiography, says, "Human felicity is produced not so much by great pieces of good fortune that seldom happen, as by little advantages that occur every day" (Franklin et al., 1981).

All in all, defining who you are is vital for personal growth, self-acceptance, and meaningful connections. It empowers you to live authentically and pursue a purpose-driven life that ultimately contributes to your overall happiness and well-being.

How to Define Who You Are?

Knowing who you are seems easy enough in theory, but in reality, is one of the hardest things people struggle to define. We are all constantly overloaded with opinions and outside ideas from friends, coworkers, and not just media but social media.

With the advances in technology that have provided us with unbound access to outside ideas, it is harder than ever before to be alone with your own thoughts and form opinions that are truly yours and yours alone. This makes defining who you are a lot more difficult than meets the eye.

To break the shackles that hold you back, you need to let go of the characteristics that undermine your confidence.

However, the real question is: How?

By understanding that you are not what your depressed mind and dark thoughts tell you.

Tell yourself:

- You are not a people pleaser.

- You are not defined solely by others' opinions.

- You are not afraid of change.

- You are not limited by fear.

- You are not defined by your past mistakes.

Take 15 minutes of your time and think deeply about WHAT YOU ARE NOT. Define what you can SAY NO to today SO THAT YOU CAN SAY YES to the right things. By understanding this and letting go of these fears, you'll naturally spring up like a new flower bud that's beginning its new path to happiness.

The process of defining who you are is an intricate and deeply personal endeavor that consists of your beliefs, values, experiences, and aspirations. It is a reflection of your unique combination of qualities and characteristics that shape your identity and distinguish you from others. Reflecting on your past experiences and extracting the lessons learned helps uncover your strengths, weaknesses, and passions, offering insights into what drives you.

Path to Happiness—Exploring Your Inner Landscape

Self-defining is an ongoing and dynamic process. It requires self-reflection, introspection, and an openness to change.

To embrace the complexity of your individuality and embrace the journey of self-discovery, you need to open yourself to new challenges in life. Learn to accept the art of change and be alone with yourself. Being alone for some time gives you space to rethink and reflect so you can realize who you are from the inside.

You can do several things to know your inner self. Some of them are mentioned in this chapter. Read on to find out how.

Identify the Layers of Your Identity

Our identity is not a single-function system like robots, but as humans, we are made of complex mixtures of emotions. Our personality traits, how we act, and what we like and dislike, all depend upon the people we meet and live with.

According to Manu C. R. Legein-Vandenhoeck, our identity is a seven-layered framework, each of which contributes to our selfhood (C. R. Legein-Vandenhoeck, n.d.).

These seven layers include:

- Body: Your mental, physical, emotional, and spiritual aspects combine to form the first layer of your identity. In any distress, your body is the first to react. Similarly, self-care for your body and mind is the first step toward happiness. By doing exercise, self-care, eating healthy, and having peace of mind, your body instantly feels positive vibes and positive changes.

- Emotions: Emotions play a crucial role in defining happiness. They are the subjective experiences that color our lives, influencing our perceptions, reactions, and overall well-being. Understanding and managing our emotions can greatly impact our ability to experience and cultivate happiness in our lives.

- Ego: *Ego in self-love* refers to "the center of power you hold over yourself." This points to a delicate yet healthy balance of the *I am* mindset and your self-esteem. A positive ego defines happiness by fostering self-confidence, self-worth, and a healthy sense of self-esteem. It allows individuals to embrace their strengths, pursue their goals, and experience fulfillment, while still maintaining humility and respect for others.

- Love: Our relationship makes a strong part of our identity. Whether you live with them for years or it's a few minutes encounter, people do leave you with long-lasting impressions that unknowingly become a part of your personality. Therefore, surrounding yourself with positive and happy people will instantly make you happy from within. You've likely heard the phrase: *you are what you eat* and in that same tone you are also the culmination of your 5 closest relationships. So if your closest friends or loved ones are unhappy, inauthentic or angry at the world you are likely to be as well.

- Speaking—communication: Effective communication forms the foundation of happiness. It fosters understanding, connection, and empathy, enabling the expression of thoughts, emotions, and needs. Through genuine and meaningful conversations, we build relationships, resolve conflicts, and share joy, ultimately enhancing our overall well-being and satisfaction in life.

- Seeing—perspective: Seeing happiness is all about perspective. It's about recognizing and appreciating the positive aspects of life, finding joy in the little things, and embracing a grateful attitude. By shifting our perspective, we can unlock happiness in even the simplest moments.

- Knowing—self-awareness: Self-awareness defines happiness by allowing individuals to understand their values, passions, and beliefs, align their actions accordingly, and make choices that lead to a more authentic and fulfilling life. It enables individuals to live in alignment with their true selves, promoting a sense of contentment and well-being.

Reflect on Your True Desires

Self-reflection is one of the fundamental pillars of happiness. It is defined as "meditating or reflecting with serious thoughts about one's true self, character, actions, and motives." A quick tip, whenever you feel, down is to take a step back and reflect on your life. Ask yourself:

- What do you want in life?

- What brings you joy and fulfillment?

- What can you do to feel happy?

Reflecting on your true desires defines happiness by examining what brings you joy and fulfillment. It involves identifying your core values and principles and understanding what truly matters to you. Additionally, recognizing your unique strengths and qualities helps you leverage them to pursue meaningful goals.

By aligning your actions and choices with your authentic desires, you can create a life that resonates with your true self, leading to a deeper sense of contentment, purpose, and lasting happiness.

How to Self-Reflect?

Self-reflection is not a complicated process that you need to fear. To make things easier, here is a four-step process that you can follow to start your self-reflection journey today:

1. Step 1—Stop: Take a step back from your life or whatever it is that is disturbing you.

2. Step 2—Look: Analyze the situation in a bigger picture. Get more than one perspective of the situation.

3. Step 3—Listen: Listen to what your mind, heart, and body are telling you.

4. Step 4—Act: After complete analysis, take steps that help to move forward and adjust to the change with a positive mindset.

Defining You by Defining What You Are Not

What makes you, *you*? This is a simple question but probably with the most difficult answer. You would have come across this once or twice in life yourself. Most people don't even know how to contemplate this question, let alone answer it. However, to take your first step toward happiness, answering this question is important. How? By defining who you are not!

Defining who you are often involves exploring what you are not. It's a process of self-discovery that requires acknowledging and letting go of societal expectations, external pressures, and limiting beliefs that don't align with your true essence.

By defining what you are not, you gain clarity about your boundaries, values, and aspirations. It empowers you to shed the layers of conformity and embrace your unique identity. This journey of self-definition liberates you from the constraints of others' opinions and allows you to authentically express yourself. By understanding what you are not, you pave the way to becoming the most genuine, fulfilled version of yourself.

Here's a checklist that can help you define what you are not:

You Are Not a People Pleaser
People pleasing is one of the factors that constantly drains us of energy and happiness. When you constantly prioritize others' needs and opinions

over your own, you automatically end up neglecting your well-being desires. Shifting away from people pleasing produces a major paradigm shift in the way you perceive things and how you take in situations.

By doing so, you reclaim your autonomy and set healthy boundaries for yourself. This enables you to focus on self-care, pursue your passions, and make choices aligned with your values. It may initially feel uncomfortable, but authentically asserting yourself fosters self-respect and genuine connections. Prioritizing your own happiness cultivates a sense of fulfillment and allows you to live a more authentic, balanced life. Remember, taking care of yourself is not selfish; it is an essential component of your overall well-being.

You Don't Need External Validation

Not needing external validation is a powerful path to happiness. When you rely solely on internal validation, you free yourself from the unpredictable judgments and opinions of others. It enables you to cultivate a deep sense of self-worth and confidence that isn't swayed by external factors.

By embracing your personal opinions and choices, you become the author of your happiness, unaffected by the approval or disapproval of others.

This inner strength allows you to make authentic decisions, pursue your passions, and live in alignment with your values.

Ultimately, by seeking validation from within, you create a sustainable and unshakeable foundation for lasting happiness and fulfillment. However, if you find yourself constantly looking for validation from outside sources or social media, it is a sign to step back and detox yourself from what can easily be a place of negative thoughts and energy.

Learn to Overcome Your Past Mistakes

Your past doesn't define you! To move ahead in life, you need to accept this reality. Learning to overcome your past mistakes allows you to release the burdens of guilt and regret, freeing your mind and spirit. By embracing the lessons learned from those mistakes, you gain wisdom and personal growth.

Forgiving yourself and cultivating self-compassion leads to inner peace and contentment. Instead of dwelling on the past, you can focus on the present and future, making better choices that align with your values. Letting go of the weight of past mistakes empowers you to live a happier, more fulfilling life.

Embrace Change and Let Go of the Fear

Change is an inherent part of life, and resisting it breeds only anxiety and discontent. By embracing change, you open yourself to new experiences, growth, and opportunities. Letting go of fear allows you to step out of your comfort zone, unleash your potential, and cultivate resilience. It frees you from the shackles of uncertainty, empowering you to adapt, thrive, and find joy in the ever-evolving journey of life. Happiness flourishes when you embrace change with courage and an open heart.

The Power of Saying No

People pleasing is a parasite that eats you from within unless and until you learn to say no. The power this word holds is impossible to express in words here. By learning to say *no*, you set up a safe zone for yourself. This means you are setting boundaries for yourself by prioritizing your self-care—and this is not unhealthy!

The power of saying no lies in its ability to honor your authentic self. By identifying what doesn't align with your values, desires, and priorities, you can protect your well-being and create a life that reflects your true essence.

Learning to say no with confidence and assertiveness enables you to set boundaries, preserve your time and energy, and avoid over-commitment (sy@dmin, 2022). By doing so, you create space for the right opportunities and experiences that truly resonate with your aspirations, leading to a more fulfilling and balanced life. Saying no becomes a powerful act of self-care, empowering you to prioritize what truly matters and cultivate happiness on your own terms.

Practice Self-Reflection Exercises

Self-reflection exercises can be highly beneficial for personal growth and can contribute significantly to the path to happiness. Here are several ways in which self-reflection exercises can help you to stay happy and positive:

- Journaling: Documenting and writing down your thoughts, ideas, and emotions is a great way to process what you are going through. This, in turn, would help you to give a clear picture of what you want and don't want. For a beginner, journaling is a great way to self-reflect.

- Guided meditation: Guided meditation promotes self-reflection for happiness by providing a focused and calming environment to explore thoughts and emotions. It cultivates mindfulness, enhances self-awareness, and allows for deep introspection, facilitating personal growth and the development of a positive mindset.

- Seeking positive feedback: Seeking feedback and insights from trusted individuals broadens perspective, uncovers blind spots, and deepens self-reflection. Their input offers valuable insights, challenges assumptions, and promotes personal growth, leading to greater self-awareness and happiness.

Embracing Your Authentic Self

Embracing your authentic self is a powerful catalyst for finding happiness and fulfillment. It involves recognizing and embracing your unique qualities and quirks and understanding that they contribute to your individuality and make you special. Honoring your values and living in alignment with them allows you to lead a life that feels true to who you are, promoting a sense of integrity and purpose.

Cultivating self-acceptance and self-compassion is also crucial in embracing your authentic self. It means recognizing that imperfections and mistakes are part of being human and treating yourself with kindness and understanding.

Plus, allowing your authentic self to shine in relationships and endeavors is liberating and empowering. By expressing your true thoughts, emotions, and desires, you attract people and opportunities that align with your authentic self. This leads to deeper connections and a greater sense of belonging and satisfaction.

Embracing your authentic self requires courage and vulnerability, but it opens the door to a more meaningful and joyful existence. By embracing who you truly are, you create a solid foundation for happiness and well-being.

Overcoming Challenges Leads to Positive Mindset

Challenges are an important part of the self-growth journey. In my travels around the world to study happy people and cultures one thing I have seen is the power that physical and mental challenges play in happiness. Some of my own happiest moments have come after incredibly difficult physical or mental challenges in which both my body and mind have to work together to overcome an obstacle. In my case this is often scaling a mountain peak, competing in an adventure race or traveling solo to far flung and remote location.

You certainly don't need to go hike Mt Everest, but setting small and large goals to challenge yourself mentally and physically are keys to lifelong happiness. Pick a few small short term challenges, and a few longer term large challenges to add into your life. Something you could do every day; like learning a language, taking a boxing class, jogging a few flights of stairs or learning a new skill and a longer term challenge like a running race, a solo trip, or an adventure activity that tests your endurance and your mental strength and requires some training to get you prepared. Whatever you decide, overcoming challenges is instrumental in cultivating a positive mindset and paving the path to happiness and success.

When you challenge yourself you break societal expectations and judgment, allowing you to embrace your true self. Succeed or fail in the challenge, you are building resilience in the face of criticism or rejection which is helping you develop inner strength and a belief in your abilities.

Moreover, seeking support and finding a community that celebrates your authenticity nurtures a sense of belonging and uplifts your spirits. As you continuously evolve and grow, exploring new aspects of yourself, you foster personal development and unlock a deeper sense of fulfillment.

Key Takeaway

The journey to self-discovery and finding your own path toward happiness is no easy task. It involves facing the sides of yourself that you have been avoiding for a long time. However, little effort and baby steps can make things a piece of cake if you start exploring the power of authenticity. When you start doing so, you'll see that authenticity has its own addiction. This addiction then leads you to happiness and fulfillment!

Exercises

Exercise 1: Defining Your Authentic Self

Self-reflection is based on valuing your beliefs and passion. Start with small things. Take a jar and drop a small note in it every day about anything. For example:

- something that made you happy

- one quality of yours that you found to be unique

- your strengths

- what brings you joy and fulfillment etc.

Then, take time to reflect on things and use these notes to define your authentic self! If you are feeling down, reach in the jar and find one of your positive affirmations and remind yourself of how awesome you are!

Exercise 2: Exploring Your Inner Landscape

Writing down goals and repeating them puts them into our psyche, and the more we think about them, the more we subconsciously work toward them.

Start writing down your thoughts and emotions rather than pushing them under the rug.

Ask yourself deep questions like, "What do I really want in life?" "What are my goals?" Or, "What are my deepest fears and aspirations?" Journal them down to build stronger insights into life and your goals. All this will ultimately lead you to happiness!

Exercise 3: Recognizing Who You Are Not

Make a checklist of all the traits or behaviors you think don't align with your authentic self, like people pleasing or seeking validation. Work on these traits one by one so that you can get rid of them. Doing so will help you shine with your true authentic self. By doing this, you can also practice self-compassion and let go of others' expectations.

Exercise 4: Saying No to the Wrong Things

Instead of always being available to others, learn to say "No." Always evaluate your commitments and activities before taking up anything that you don't want to do. Identify the obligations that drain you out. Set your priorities and work on them. Anything other than that is extra! You don't have to do that extra when you already have too much on your plate. By saying no to the wrong things, you create space to say yes to the right opportunities and experiences.

Chapter 2: Goals—Mapping Your Path to Happiness

Do you know the difference between people who are successful and happy and those who are not? If you ask them, successful and happy people will never give vague responses like, "I was just riding the waves of life when one day magic happened. I started thriving, and life became blissful."

No, their stories will always detail the steps they took and the dedication they showed to create the magic themselves! Simply put, the people you see prospering in this world are those with dreams and the goals and plan to make them happen.

The ideal way to work toward a goal is by answering the *why* question for ourselves. Friedrich Nietzsche once said, "He who has a why to live can bear almost any how." Once you're clear on the driving force behind that cherished goal, everything else will fall into place.

So, why that specific goal? Why do you want it so badly? Why did you purchase this book to help you achieve it? The key is to figure out why you truly want what you want, and you'll automatically be driven to focus on how you're going to achieve it.

This chapter is all about how to set and achieve these goals in life to embark on the road to happiness. So let's see how below!

Importance of Setting Goals

I cannot emphasize enough the importance of keeping and maintaining goals in your life every step of the way. Have you ever worked super hard toward something? Do you remember the dopamine rush, the feeling of pure bliss once you achieved that thing? This is what the purpose of goals is in our lives.

Setting small, achievable goals will help you witness those small victories and give you a sense of success that you're getting nearer and nearer to achieving your big dream!

Imagine you're starting a hike up a mountain, you have no shoes, no gear and no path. Without a defined path, trail, or any signposts, you won't have any idea where the summit is. You'll be wandering aimlessly without any sense of direction, unable to reach the finish point.

Goals serve as the trail or the signposts that will lead you to the summit. By defining and clarifying what we want to achieve, goals provide us with a sense of purpose and direction to help navigate us toward our big goal.

The Art of Goal Setting

The reason we're calling it *the art* of goal setting is because defining your goals is not as simple as it sounds. If you're thinking, *I want to buy a car, I want to lose weight,* or *I want to travel the world*, then you're thinking wrong.

Goals are not just about the final outcome. Setting goals goes beyond simply dreaming of the success you want. It's a deliberate and evolving process that sets down a timeline, defines objectives, and carves a specific path toward the end goal.

Understanding the Differences Between
Random Desires and Well-Defined Goals

Before finalizing your goal, you must be able to distinguish between random mundane wishes and concrete achievements. There are several key differences between the two.

For instance, if what you're considering to be a goal lacks clarity and motivation, is devoid of an action plan, or lacks conscious intention behind it, then it's not a goal. Rather, it's a fleeting desire.

A goal has concrete intentions. It's something you've thought about, something you have a substantial plan for, and it strongly roots itself in your consciousness till it becomes a reality.

Unlike random desires, goals have a direction and concrete steps to be taken in order to move closer to achieving the goal.

So, for example, if a goal makes you think, *I want to travel more*, it's not a goal but a mere temporary desire. However, if by the goal you're thinking, *I want to visit five new countries within the next three years*, this is a goal clearly defined with a concrete idea of what must be achieved. It demands a plan and the establishment of smaller goals like researching destinations, gathering funds, etc., which will build up to the final success.

The SMART Criteria for Effective Goal Setting

It can be difficult to filter out your temporary desires from your goals at once. It is common and completely okay to confuse the two. However, there are certain tools, such as SMART, which help in the effective goal setting. The acronym stands for Specific, Measurable, Achievable, Relevant, and Time-bound.

- Specific: Goals have no room for ambiguity. They must be precise and specific and answer all the when's, whys, how's, where's, what's, etc. The more well-defined you make your goal, the more likely you are to successfully achieve it.

- Measurable: The very point of having a goal is to work toward achieving it at all costs. As such, your goal must be measurable. You must think of objective indicators to measure your progress.

- Achievable: Achieving does not mean you should stop challenging yourself. After all, goals are all about accomplishing what isn't easily attainable. However, you must make sure that the goal is within the realm of possibilities and the resources available to you.

- Relevant: You will only work toward and achieve your goal when you're personally connected to it. Your goal should be relevant to your aspirations, values, and objectives.

- Time-bound: It is extremely crucial that your goal is time-bound. Deadlines and time frames are the biggest motivators that push you to work and consequently achieve. Giving yourself a time frame will create urgency and positive pressure and force you to prioritize relevant tasks. It will ensure that you stay on track toward achieving your goal.

Breaking Down Big Goals Into Smaller

Actionable Steps

Your ambitious goals can become overwhelming. They can lead you into confusion, wondering where you start, how you even begin, or what should be the first step. This is why it always helps to break down the big goal into smaller actionable goals that build toward the grand finale.

Once you break down the goals into different steps, the process becomes more manageable and less daunting. Plus, with achievable tasks, you feel better driven to exert your energies into achieving the goal.

In order to break down the big goal into smaller ones, you must work backward. Think of the end goal you want to achieve. What resources do you need? What steps must be taken? How will you end up there?

With these questions in mind, start jotting down the small milestones or tasks you need to achieve to get closer to tasting your end goal.

Aligning Goals With Your Values and Authentic Self

The only way your goals will hold any meaning or satisfaction for you is if they align with your values and beliefs. An empty goal that does not connect with you will only become a burden.

The reason it's so important to align your goals with your values is that it will fuel your motivation and passion to work rigorously to achieve the goal. This connection between yourself, your values, and your goal is what will keep you strong and persistent in the face of challenges.

Think about the most important values to you, the morals and principles that you hold dear, the beliefs that calm you, and the aspirations and interests that make your heart beat faster.

Once you have identified what matters to you, the external societal pressures disguising themselves as your goals will fall off your mind, leaving behind only what you truly want.

Discovering Your *Why*

In order to truly achieve success and happiness, your goals must be fueled by a *why*. Think about why you want to do or achieve that particular thing. Why is attaining a particular goal so important to you?

Our *why* is often fueled by a deeper motivation. The process of uncovering the deeper motivation behind your goals brings you face-to-face with your intrinsic inspirations. These are the secret driving force behind your goal. Staying in touch with your deeper motivation for the goal will sustain your interest and give you the energy to remain persistent in achieving that goal.

Moreover, the process of identifying the purpose and meaning behind your aspirations involves self-reflection and engaging in a deeper comprehension of your values, desires, and interests.

The moment you figure out why you're driven to achieve a certain goal, your aspirations, goals, and you become one. This harmony is a phenomenal combination that can lead you to fulfilling your dreams and goals.

It is also important to understand that true happiness and success stem from knowing that you achieved what you were the most passionate about. Hence, it's crucial to connect your goals to your core values and passion. When you align your goal with something as crucial as that, it transforms the goal into something inexplicably meaningful.

So, ask yourself what is this goal for. Is it for you, or are you trying to merely please someone else? Why is it so important to you? How are you connected to this goal?

Smaller Goals—A Step Toward a Bigger Achievement

It is a natural human instinct to directly aim for a step without realizing the downfalls. Or else we try to take shortcuts to our desired goal. Both of these strategies are bound to land you in despair and failure in the end. Therefore, smaller goals and baby steps to the actual goal is always the best option!

Smaller actionable milestones keep you on track. Your short-term goals ultimately contribute to your long-term vision. Think of these short goals as pieces of your big goal. You must pick up all the pieces on the way and keep putting them together. Eventually, you'll start seeing the picture you envisioned.

Also, a logical sequence to the smaller goals is extremely important. Without that, the smaller goals will get mixed up, complicating your path. So, if your goal is to buy a car, your first small goal will not be to place a token on your dream. You will figure out the finances first and devise a plan and timeline to gather enough funds before you even plan a visit to the showroom.

How to Plan These Short-Term Goals

The easiest way to plan and succeed with this strategy is to create a timeline and an action plan for each goal! This is a harsh truth that without a fixed timeline and specific deadlines, you will be stuck on the first few steps only for a lengthy amount of time. Deadlines are the motivating factor. They prevent you from wasting away precious time and resources with the *I'll eventually get to it* attitude.

Plus, tracking your progress over time helps you stay focused. Until you track your progress, you will not know where you stand, how far along you are, or how much of the journey is still left. So, make sure you have indicators to objectively measure your progress.

Not only will this be a source of motivation when you figure out how far along you've come, but it will also allow you to tweak your schedule or pick up—slow down—your pace based on how much you have been able to achieve.

Visualizing Success With Goals

Nothing can stop you from achieving your goal once you've visualized the details of the moment when you have it all. The reason is that once you've tasted sweet victory, even just in your imagination, the desire for it significantly escalates, till you experience it again, for real.

Harnessing the power of the mental picturization of achieving your goal is the perfect means of igniting a never-ending fire of motivation within you. Seeing what you can achieve encourages you to work for it harder. In fact, you will experience a confidence and motivation boost like you've never experienced before.

The process is fairly simple. Situate yourself in a quiet, calming, and relaxing place. Visualize the moment you finally achieve your goal. Imagine it with as much clarity and detail as you're capable of. What are you doing? Who is with you? Where are you? What are you wearing? Picture every minor and major detail.

I know I haven't shared a lot of personal stories in this book, so let me share one now on visualization. In my youth, I was a competitive gymnast. On a daily basis, I was performing difficult maneuvers with my body that defied gravity. While the physical side was hard, it was the mental part I had to master in order to succeed. Every practice and every evening, I spent moments visualizing the skills I was about to do and the ones I wanted to learn. Over and over in my mind, I performed the skill until I did it perfectly every time. If I fell in my mind, I rewrote the memory again and again with perfection so that my mind already mastered and believed I could do it.

The visualization strategy is not a one-time thing. For this process to work, you must incorporate it into your daily routine. Or, at least perform this exercise as regularly as you can.

The more you practice, the more you will notice a rise in your passion and motivation to finish what you started growing gradually.

The Role of Accountability

Achieving your goals, finding happiness, or attaining success for yourself are all very individual processes. While they may involve other loved or cherished ones, the driving force is you alone. So, without anyone forcing you to work toward your goals, it can be difficult to perform consistently. As such, you must take accountability.

While you will be the one calling all the shots when it comes to planning out your goal, it can help to have external support like a trusted friend or a family member. Accountability partnerships or masterminds can also help you to monitor yourself. This network allows you to support, guide, and hold each other accountable in the process of achieving your goals.

Along with all this, always keep track of your progress. Keep tabs on the milestones achieved, tasks left, and the pace at which you're working. Tracking your progress will not only make you more efficient and allow you to tweak the action plan but also keep you on your toes and motivated.

Overcoming Obstacles and Resilience

Obstacles and resilience are part and parcel of the self-awareness journey and achieving your goals. Never think of them as interference. Rather, these are the learning curves that impart unparalleled wisdom. Although, they can indeed put a damper on things. So, it is important to keep an attitude that doesn't let challenges bring you down.

The right approach to handling obstacles and setbacks is to always anticipate them. Always keep your action plans flexible. Make a note of any potential thing that could go wrong and make a contingency plan for it. You may never have to use it, but just in case you do, it will save you from being stuck and wasting time.

Furthermore, developing resilience and persistence is the key to dealing with these obstacles. There is no doubt that these challenges are the test of your persistence, dedication, and passion toward achieving your goal. However, by being focused and steadfast, happiness is sure to come!

As cliché as it may sound, setbacks are a fantastic learning opportunity! They teach you lessons that you can apply to a number of different situations because they teach you to think on your feet and work under pressure.

Lastly, always seek help when you get stuck. Do not deny yourself the comfort of trusted friends, mentors, family, or other support networks. The best ideas to overcome obstacles can come from anywhere and anyone. You never know; some obstacles could even end up being a blessing in disguise! A saying I love, is *Life is happening For you, not to you.* Think about obstacles and events in your life as a stepping stone to something else, rather than a negative.

Reflection and Adjustment of Goals

The path to achieving your goal is not straight or unchanging. It evolves as you work toward this goal. So, it is crucial to be flexible and open to reflections and making adjustments to your plans.

In fact, reflection and adjustment are the compass and map that guide us toward the shores of lasting happiness. Picture a goalkeeper on a soccer field. With every incoming ball, they analyze, adapt, and make split-second decisions. Similarly, in life, we must pause, reflect, and adjust our goals to align them with our authentic selves.

Moreover, reflection offers us the precious opportunity to question our aspirations and assess their true worth. It allows us to uncover our deepest desires, separating societal expectations from our genuine passions. Through introspection, we gain clarity about what truly brings us joy, enabling us to set meaningful and fulfilling goals.

But reflection alone is not enough. It is the humble act of adjustment that transforms reflection into a catalyst for happiness. Just as a goalkeeper adapts their position to meet each new challenge, we must be willing to modify our goals when necessary. Life is an ever-evolving game, and our goals must evolve with it. By remaining open-minded and flexible, we increase our chances of finding contentment and fulfillment.

Key Takeaway

The bottom line is, your happiness and success are tied to realizing and defining what truly matters to you. Once you figure out what you're most passionate about, you need to turn that into an achievable, time-bound goal and work diligently to achieve it. This sense of purpose and working toward something will give meaning to your life and lead you to the happiness you so desire.

In addition, purposeful goal setting provides us with direction and a sense of purpose. It fuels our motivation to do more and more. This is not just a journey of happiness and success but also personal growth and a deepening connection to our authentic selves.

Exercises

Exercise 1: Setting S.M.A.R.T. Goals

The best way to go about setting SMART goals is to take them out of your head and write them down so they're always in front of you. Make a Dreams & Goals journal to roadmap your journey to success and happiness. Make a note of the following in the journal:

- Your long-term dreams and goals.

- For each goal, define smaller achievable goals that you can start acting on.

- Make sure to use the SMART tool. For instance, define indicators and a time frame within which you expect to achieve the goal.

Keep adding to the journal every day. Add new goals, tweak older ones, and checkmark the things you've accomplished. Pro tip? For every task, write down a way to reward yourself when you achieve it, and make sure to do it once the task is done!

Exercise 2: Saying No So You Can Say Yes

In order to achieve your goals, you must eliminate things from your life that hold you back and exhaust you. Practice saying no to what's unimportant so you can say yes to success and happiness.

Take a piece of paper and fold it in half to make columns. You can do this exercise in your dreams and goals journal as well. Simply divide the paper into two sections by drawing a line down the middle.

On one side of the paper, state your dreams and goals. On the other side, write down every activity you do on a normal day. Work, extra hours watching TV, using the phone, etc. Now, cross off anything that unnecessarily consumes your energy, makes you unhappy, or pulls you away from your dream or goal listed on the left.

Do this exercise for each goal in your journal. By eliminating these activities, you will have more time and energy to finish your stepping stone goals and be able to get what you want sooner.

Exercise 3: Visualizing Your Why

It is very important to connect to the root cause of your goal. The best way to do that is to visualize every reason that motivates you to chase after a particular goal.

Create a vision board for yourself. Get a chart paper or a board. At the center of it, write down your long-term goal—dream. Around this dream, branch out every reason why you want to achieve the goal.

Use clippings, pictures, poetry, quotes, symbols, and anything that connects you to the reason for this goal on a deeper level. Add to the board whenever you can and keep it somewhere so your eyes will always fall on it.

Every day, take time out to look at the board and allow yourself to form a connection with every reason you've jotted down. Spend some quiet minutes looking at the vision in front of you and instill all the whys in your core.

Exercise 4: Writing Down and Displaying Your Goals

Just like visualizing your why is important, having your goal written in front of you where you can see it at all times is also crucial. In our busy days, it is important to not let ourselves forget our purpose and goals.

So, the easiest trick for this is to get a stack of sticky notes. Be creative, get different shapes and colors. On each sticky note, write down the long-term goals that keep you up at night or get you daydreaming.

Place these sticky notes on your mirror, cupboard, or any other visible place. Arrange them in order of priority and keep them as reminders.

Exercise 5: Reviewing and Adjusting Your Goals

To ensure progress toward the completion of your goal and the consequent success and happiness, you must perform constant reviews and adjustments. Here is where a Dreams & Goals journal will help you.

Detail your long-term goals, their subsequent smaller and achievable goals, a timeframe and deadlines, and other nitty-gritty of achieving the goal. Make sure to set at least 10–15 minutes aside every day or every other day to review the journal.

Mark down the accomplishments and achievements you've made. Track your progress and make adjustments to the plan based on your current pace.

Chapter 3: Affirmations and Vision Boarding—Harnessing the Power of Positivity

You must have heard the phrase: "You are what you eat." Take it out of the context of food, and you are everything you feed yourself. Everything that enters your head, every word, image, scenario, emotion, reaction, registers and stays in your mind. All these things set in your brain also have the power to change your thoughts and attitudes about the way you live your life.

So, whether it is confidence or insecurity, positivity or negativity, happiness or gloom, whatever you feed yourself, you become it. That is why the first step to success becomes being kind to yourself and absorbing nothing but positivity! Shun the negativity. Make sure there is no room for it in your head.

The best way to remain focused is to think about your goal and why you want to achieve it. Vividly imagine it in your mind with so much detail as if you are in the moment and you've finally achieved it. Once you feel the indescribable happiness within you, open your eyes. Remind yourself that only positivity and powerful happy thoughts can help you get there.

The Power of Positivity

Did you know that positive people are 13% less likely to suffer from heart attacks? (Johns Hopkins Medicine, 2019). Just imagine the extent of the power of positive thinking. If positivity can keep you this healthy, it could definitely drive you to immense success and happiness.

Here's a little story. In my early twenties, I found myself in a negative rut. I was going through a breakup, had no job, and was generally very unhappy with my life's circumstances. Everything felt wrong, and I couldn't find any solution to my problems and eventually, sadness snuck in. That is when one of my friends offered some advice.

She recommended that I think positively no matter the situation. That I put a smile on face, high five myself in the mirror when I wake up and even when things seem grim to try to see the positivity in me and in being alive. She said, "Think positively no matter how bad the situation is. Even if you're on your deathbed, just think positively. Because nothing happens without a good reason, and we are our the creators of our own destiny."

That is when I started rethinking my life circumstances and realized that I needed to stop blaming others for my problems, stop being hopeless and start living life like I was already happy, even though I wasn't quite there yet. This mindset shift from a negative pattern of thoughts to a more positive one, took time, but soon I was making positive steps forward to make my life better, get rid of toxic people and see life through a new perspective. There are still moments in which I may feel down, but now I am a very happy person, and know that my energy and outward joy for life is contagious to all those that I am around. So many of our problems are self-generated, taking accountability for that and changing our mindset towards positivity can absolutely change your situation. Embrace it.

Know that your thoughts affect your actions, and your actions determine whether or not you attain success (Robbins, n.d.). I know several people that have been so stuck in negative thoughts that all they receive are negative events. Constantly consuming negative news and ideas, their entire mind has been changed, and finding positivity and goodness has become almost impossible. Do not let this happen to you. Motivational self-talk and controlling your thoughts go a long way in creating a positive aura around you.

Try following this simple list of positivity:

- Practice catching yourself mid-negative thoughts, and turn them around by focusing on something positive. Delayed flight? Instead of focusing on the time spent waiting, do something constructive or think about how you are finally safely on the plane on your way.

- Stop blaming yourself for bad situations. Everyone runs into a dump every now and then. Keep a solution-oriented mindset, instead of a woe is me attitude.

- Be conscious of your vocabulary. Replace your negative words and phrases with positive ones.

Empower yourself through positive talk and affirmations every day. Don't just think about them in your head. Give your thoughts life through spoken words. "I am happy today," "Today is a good day," "I am focusing on the positivity," and, "I am confident and smart." Speaking such empowering phrases to yourself and anticipating positivity has the power to attract good to you.

Affirmations: Rewriting Your Inner Narrative

Affirmations are "phrases meant to be repeated and instilled in oneself to combat negative thought patterns" (Goldman & Young, 2022). *Positive affirmations* are "a form of self-help. They are meant to instill confidence and self-esteem in yourself, reduce fear and self-sabotaging tendencies, and most of all, cheer you up, especially in difficult situations" (Taylor, 2022).

It is extremely important to consciously choose positive affirmations for yourself to achieve happiness and success in any area of life. Positive affirmations work best when you craft them specifically, according to your goals, personality, traits, and situation in life. Your affirmations should resonate with you. There are many ways you can go about it:

- Think of a quality, trait, or decision you made and highlight every positive aspect of it to yourself.

- Repeat positive affirmations to yourself like, "I am worthy of love, happiness, and success," "I control my own happiness," "My hard work will pay off," etc.

- In your dreams and goals journal, write down your core values, positive thoughts, positive decisions you took, positive reactions you had, etc.

- Change your attitude. Remember that the world is abundant with opportunity, money, happiness and success. Keep a growth mindset by adjusting and adapting to the situation.

However, positive affirmations will only work if you surround yourself with them. Defeat the skepticism when you feel silly lying in bed or standing in front of a mirror telling yourself you're strong. Believe in every word you tell yourself, repeat positive phrases daily, and write them down and display them around so you have them in plain sight to remind you. Surround yourself with the reminders of what you want will help you get there sooner.

The Science Behind Affirmations

Affirmations have a substantial impact on the subconscious mind, and science proves it! In fact, affirmations, in a way, reprogram the subconscious mind to overwrite other negative thoughts. But how?

Our brains have evolved to think quickly and make snap decisions for survival, given that analytical decision-making takes time. Hence, our brains are constantly creating shortcuts that result in cognitive biases (*The Science Behind Positive Affirmations*, 2021).

When you repeat affirmations to yourself, the brain's neural pathways fire up and trigger the areas of the brain that A) make you happy and B) create a cognitive bias (*The Science Behind Positive Affirmations*, 2021). So, your brain subconsciously starts looking for signs and noticing things that could help make your affirmation come true. Additionally, the brain presents these affirmations to the conscious mind as well, leading you to notice opportunities that will help achieve your goal!

Moreover, a study has been published on this phenomenon in the Social Cognitive and Affective Neuroscience journal that proves the connection between self-affirmations and the activation of reward centers in the brain (*The Science Behind Positive Affirmations*, 2021).

Practicing Affirmations

In order for affirmations to work, you must create an environment conducive to them and dedicatedly practice them. For instance, incorporate different kinds of affirmations in your everyday routine.

Practice spoken affirmations before you start your day by vocalizing your positive thoughts to yourself aloud. Write down positive affirmations and keep them around you on your mirror, side table, kitchen, office desk, etc. Visualize your positive thoughts, see the change you want to actualize in your head first, and vividly.

Several meditation and visualization exercises incorporate affirmations. For instance:

- Affirmation breathing: Sit down in a calm and relaxing environment that brings you comfort and feels safe. Choose a positive affirmation of the day. Relax your body and begin slowly inhaling. With every inhalation, repeat the affirmation in your head. As you exhale slowly, release all the doubts, skepticism, and negative thoughts.

- Visualization and affirmation: You can practice this exercise as you go to sleep. Close your eyes and visualize an affirmation. See what you want to believe and create in the world. As you picture it behind closed eyelids, repeat the affirmations to yourself in your head.

Affirmations can be applied to different aspects of your life. You can reprogram your thoughts about friends, family, career, relationships, health, finances, and any other area. The key is to figure out what you want, devise positive affirmations in those areas, repeat that to yourself, and believe you are capable of achieving it (Gladnapp, 2019).

Vision Boarding: Manifesting Your Desires

Vision boards serve as a powerful visual representation tool involving your desires, goals, and dreams. This creative tool uses pictures, words, magazine–newspaper clippings, quotes, poetry, and any other symbol of your goal to create a collage of what you want to achieve in life. Their purpose is to be a relentless reminder of your goals so you actively work to pursue them.

As such, the first step to indulging in vision boards is to define your vision. Take some time to self-reflect and identify what motivates you, what speaks to you, what is your goal, or what you most want to do in life. Once you identify a goal, gather visual representations for it. Write down positive affirmations, get pictures, etc. Create a collage of your dream with the dream itself written at the center.

So, if it's still a little overwhelming, here's how you can start creating your own vision board:

- Identify the dream you want to work on.

- Gather visual materials for your goal.

- Get a board or a chart paper and write out your goal in big bold words at the center.

- Now, arrange your visual material around this goal on the board.

- Use affirmations and words that best motivate you.

- Keep the vision board where you can never miss it.

Making the Vision the Reality

The power of the vision board comes not in just creating it, but in seeing your goals and dreams every day. These hopes and dreams when seen every day, get implanted into our psyche and little by little we subconsciously and consciously start making them into a reality. I have already mentioned the power of visualization, a mental technique wherein you picture yourself in a particular situation, living a goal or a dream you wish to achieve in life. This powerful tool engages your various senses and taps into your emotions as you visualize your goal to help you make progress in its direction.

The best part is you can integrate visualization techniques with your vision board. Once you are clear and precise with your vision or your goal, translate it on the vision board. Use affirmations that were in your head as you pictured your achievement. Add the emotions you felt, and the senses that were heightened, what did you hear, see and smell when this goal was achieved in your vision?

Visualization strengthens your belief in your ability to achieve your goals. Once you can picture it clearly in your head, you will be driven to make it a reality. However, such a powerful motivation will only come with diligent and routine visualization practice.

Bringing Affirmations and Vision Boards Together

The combined power of affirmations and vision boards can really push you to achieve your goals. As you picture your goal and translate it onto a vision board, you must also have the belief and confidence in yourself that you, of all people, are perfectly capable of achieving it. This confidence boost will come with affirmations.

Say, for example, your vision board portrays a vivid picture of achieving good health and fitness. Channel that picture into affirmations such as:

- I am dedicated to providing my body with routine exercise and healthy food.

- I have the energy and stamina needed to transform my body.

- I love and respect my body.

- Every day, I am making progress toward attaining a fit body.

It is important to be consistent and committed to exercise. Remember, your affirmations and vision boards are not unchanging. As you make progress, your affirmations may change since you are now getting closer to achieving the goal.

Another thing you can do is integrate your affirmations within the vision board. Add your positive thoughts to your vision board. As your goal evolves or you progress, change those affirmations.

Having the two together side by side will act as a persistent reminder of what you can do and where you want to invest your energies.

Integrating Affirmations and Vision Boards in Your Life

If you're up for integrating affirmations and vision boards in your life, get ready to witness a transformative experience. You are bound to notice a visible difference in the way you strive to achieve your goals and affirm your confidence and self-belief in making it through the journey.

However, this is only possible when you have identified your goal and created a vision board to visualize it. With this, the next steps to follow are simple:

- Take time out every day to connect with your goal through the vision board.

- Recite your goal and the relevant affirmations in terms of your commitment, confidence, and any other area that connects to your goal.

- Align your affirmations to your goal and make them specific.

- Chant them with conviction and louder every time a negative thought tries to distract you. Fight the *But what if-* with positive thoughts.

You must not shy away from flexibility and adaptability. Keep yourself grounded in reality and its unpredictability. As you grow and strive to achieve your goals, be open to changes and tweaks in your vision and change your affirmations accordingly.

Focus all your energy on manifesting your goal by leveraging the combined power of affirmations and vision boards. Look at the vision board with the affirmations on repeat in your head. Stay persistent and do not bow down to negativity.

Achieve Your Goals Through Affirmations and Vision Boards

Intentional self-talk, such as affirmations and constant reminders of your purpose, have the power to cultivate a go-getter and positive mindset. These tools are ways to get closer to your goal before you actually achieve it. They instill in you the confidence that you can, in fact, achieve whatever you put your mind to.

Pairing affirmations and vision boards together is a fantastic idea because it makes the journey of achieving your goal seem easier. As you build your confidence through positive self-talk and visualize your dream simultaneously, you begin to ignore the obstacles that overthinking brings into the equation. This further motivates you to work harder to achieve the goal.

In essence, in order to embrace happiness and success, you must first embrace the idea that you are not only deserving of it but very capable of achieving it. This idea will only take root in you once you boost your belief and self-confidence through affirmations, visualize your dreams, and translate them on a vision board as a persistent reminder. Something for which giving up isn't an option.

Affirmations and Vision Boarding Exercises

Exercise 1: Cultivating Positive Self-Talk Through Affirmations

Positive self-talk is the food for confidence and manifesting your goals and dreams. Making it a routine is the best decision you'll take in your life. Here's how you can go about it:

- Define a goal that resonates with you.

- Make a list of positive affirmations that are relevant to your goal.

- You can either, daily, write down these affirmations in a journal as you speak them aloud. Or simply stand in front of a mirror and speak to yourself with conviction. You must leave skepticism at the door for this to work.

- Take a moment to internalize the message you're giving yourself. Don't let your mind distract you with a negative thought; battle it with your affirmations.

Exercise 2: Visualizing Your Dream Outcome

The first step to realizing your dream is to know what you want and picture it in your head. Not only will this visualization motivate you to work for it, but on the off chance that this dream isn't a long-term one, visualization will allow you to realize it. For instance, you will not feel as passionate about it as you visualize it.

Follow these steps to visualize your goal:

1. Find a comfortable place away from distractions.

2. Sit down comfortably and take deep breaths to relax.

3. Close your eyes and start picturing your dream in your head. Visualize images, people, places, smells, sounds, and every other detail. Be specific and leave no stone unturned in your imagination.

4. Engage your emotions and senses. Feel the things you will feel at the moment; feel the tears or the smile, hear the sounds of the moment, etc.

5. Give yourself time to immerse and stay in this moment in your head.

6. Finally, open your eyes and let the feelings, emotions, and thoughts wash over you.

7. Practice this routinely for 15–20 minutes or more.

Exercise 3: Creating a Vision Board

Creating a vision board is the most fun part of achieving your dreams and goals. This step involves materializing your visualization into something tangible that you can always look at. You can be as creative as you want with your vision board; just remember to stay relevant.

1. Get a board, chart paper, card sheet, or other background material.

2. Write your goal at the very center of it in big bold letters.

3. Gather materials like pictures, magazine clippings, quotes, poetry pieces, words, and other things that relate to your goal. It could be places, colors, sounds, or anything.

4. Arrange and stick this material around your goal. You can make sections such as the place where you will achieve your goal, the people you want with you, etc.

5. Put up the vision board in a place where your eyes cannot ignore it.

6. Look at it every day and repeat your affirmations in your head for a few minutes.

7. You can make changes to the board as your goal evolves.

Exercise 4: Revisiting and Updating Your Affirmations and Vision Board

1. Define a goal or a dream for yourself. Make sure it is long-term and you have thought it through.

2. Create a vision board around your goal. Make it as creative and attractive as you can so your eyes are constantly attracted to it.

3. Make it a part of your routine to engage with your vision board. Set time aside every day, at least 10–15 minutes, to revisit your dream that is plastered on the vision board. Spend time revisiting every picture, every word, everything on the board.

4. On a designated day every week, review everything on the board and assess its relevance. Keep tabs on your progress; what things have been accomplished, what goals are yet to be achieved, and what changes have occurred.

5. Based on the progress or your personal growth, make changes to the vision board.

Remove things that no longer seem relevant, add new affirmations, change pictures, etc.

6. Keep adding visuals and words to the board. Your vision board will grow and evolve with you.

Chapter 4: Mindfulness—Cultivating Present Moment Awareness

In the hustle and bustle of our daily lives, happiness often seems like an elusive goal. We frequently find ourselves constantly chasing after the next achievement or material possession, hoping it will bring us lasting joy. But what if true happiness lies not in the future but in the present moment? That's where mindfulness and present-moment awareness comes in!

Before we move ahead, just pause for a second and think, why do we develop this habit in the first place? Many spiritual leaders and philosophers from all over the world have tried to answer this question for far, but to no legit outcome.

Instead, an impetuous high schooler from the classic 1986 movie *Ferris Bueller's Day Off* gave us the most realistic answer in the passage that stayed with us for this long. "Life moves pretty fast," he warned. "If you don't stop and look around for a while, you might miss it."

This can't be more true. Life moves pretty fast. If we spend all our lives running, we might never be able to cherish the small moments of happiness that come along with it. As said, *"When we wake up, go to work, and do the other things we need to do, we often operate on autopilot; the days fly by, as do the weeks, months, and years"* (Langshur & Klemp, 2021). That's why mindfulness and being aware in the moment are as essential as oxygen itself!

This chapter will guide you on a journey of self-discovery, offering practical steps to integrate mindfulness into your daily routine. By embracing mindfulness, you'll cultivate a deep sense of gratitude, find peace amidst chaos, and foster a genuine connection with yourself and others. So let's go!

What Is Mindfulness?

Before we learn how to be more mindful in order to achieve happiness, let's first understand the basic concept of *mindfulness*. According to the American

Psychological Association, it is "the awareness of one's internal and external states and surroundings" (*Mindfulness*, 2022).

In simpler terms, *mindfulness* is "a practice that encourages you to pay deliberate attention to your thoughts, feelings, and sensations, without judgment or attachment." Developing this heightened awareness can help you become fully present in each moment, awakening to the richness and beauty of life as it unfolds.

> Mindfulness is cultivating a non-reactive and non-judgmental awareness of one's thoughts, emotions, and sensations. By training the mind to stay focused on the present, mindfulness helps individuals break free from the grip of past regrets and future worries, leading to increased clarity and happiness (*What Is Mindfulness?*, n.d.).

It enables individuals to fully engage in and appreciate the simple joys of life, fostering gratitude and a deeper sense of contentment. By cultivating present-moment awareness, mindfulness empowers individuals to respond to life's challenges with greater resilience and equanimity, ultimately paving the way to lasting happiness.

Benefits of Mindfulness

Mindfulness might seem like a trivial thing on the road to happiness, but it offers a myriad of benefits that enhance overall well-being. By practicing present-moment awareness, individuals can change the way they think and feel in a matter of a few days (Harvard Health, 2019). Some of the well-known benefits of mindful awareness include:

- Reduces stress and anxiety.

- Enhances emotional regulation and resilience.

- Improves focus, concentration, and cognitive abilities.

- Cultivates a greater sense of compassion and self-acceptance.

- Strengthens your relationships.

- Promotes overall mental and physical health.

- Cultivates a sense of gratitude and contentment.

Key Components of Mindfulness

Mindfulness is "an integrated process that is based on three main components: intention, attention, and attitude." To effectively cultivate mindfulness, it is essential to understand these key components. By delving into these components, you'll gain a deeper understanding of how to integrate mindfulness into your daily life and experience its transformative power.

1. Intention: The first step in mindfulness is the intention of your thought. It is solely by your choice that you choose to be mindful of your surroundings and people. This is achieved by setting an intention to be there in your present rather than being stuck in your thoughts.

2. Attention: Once you build an intention to be mindful, you need to give full attention to your body and breathing. Try to comprehend how you feel about a particular situation and how you can make it better and happy for your sake.

3. Attitude: Your attitude dictates your entire process of being mindful. Therefore, it's solely up to you how you wish to make your present happy. So try having a positive attitude, as it's one of the pillars of happiness.

Practicing Mindfulness

Research done by the University of Minnesota says, *"Incorporating mindfulness into our daily lives is a powerful way to cultivate a more present and conscious existence"* (*What Is Mindfulness?*, n.d.).

In the true sense, this is essential for both a healthy mind and a healthy body. This section explores practical techniques and exercises to integrate mindfulness into our routines. Some of the techniques are:

Developing a Daily Mindfulness Routine

The consistent habit of engaging in mindful practices can help us train our minds to stay grounded in the present moment. Mindfulness cultivates a heightened sense of self-awareness, allowing you to recognize and detach from negative thought patterns and emotions.

With regular practice, mindfulness helps us develop a more positive and compassionate outlook, fostering gratitude, resilience, and a deeper appreciation for life's simple pleasures. By dedicating time each day to mindfulness, you nurture your well-being by reducing stress and opening yourself up to a more fulfilling and joyful existence.

Engaging in Formal Mindfulness Meditation Practices

We all have heard that practice makes a man perfect. However, you must be confused about how to relate this to mindfulness, right? Simple–just like any other skill!

When you set aside dedicated time to sit in meditation, you can cultivate a deepened sense of self-awareness and inner peace in yourself. Through focused attention on the breath or body sensations, meditation helps quiet the mind, reduce stress, and promote relaxation.

This allows you to observe thoughts and emotions without judgment, fostering a greater understanding of oneself. This heightened awareness and emotional regulation enable individuals to respond to life's challenges with equanimity and compassion, paving the way to a more joyful and fulfilling existence.

Incorporating Mindfulness Into Everyday Activities

Incorporating mindfulness into everyday activities is a key step on the path to happiness. By bringing mindful awareness to routine tasks such as eating, walking, and interacting with others, we cultivate a deeper appreciation for the present moment.

This practice allows us to savor the simple joys of life, reduce stress, and enhance our overall well-being. Mindfulness helps us find contentment in the ordinary, leading to a more fulfilled and joyful existence.

Common Challenges in Mindfulness Practice

While mindfulness practice can bring profound benefits, it is not without challenges. By acknowledging and addressing these obstacles, we can navigate the path of mindfulness with greater ease and deepen our practice for lasting transformation.

These challenges are:

1. Doubt

Doubt is the number one plague that often ruins your mind and destroys mindfulness. The single thought, *Would that really work for me?* is enough to ruin your weeks' effort to build a better character. The best way to deal with this doubt is to understand that thoughts are just thoughts. You should not allow them to control you; rather, you should control them. Acknowledging this fear and acting oppositely helps you come out of this feeling and ultimately puts you on a path to happiness.

2. Irritation

Irritation can pose a challenge to mindfulness practice as it disrupts your ability to stay present and centered. When irritation arises, it's crucial to approach it with mindful awareness. By acknowledging the irritation without judgment and observing its physical and emotional sensations, you can create space and distance from it.

Cultivating self-compassion and redirecting attention to the present moment through deep breathing or grounding techniques can help alleviate irritation. Additionally, practicing loving-kindness meditation can foster a sense of goodwill toward ourselves and others, reducing irritation and enhancing our ability to maintain mindfulness (Payne et al., 2021).

3. Sleepiness

The body's natural response to relaxation and stillness can often lead to drowsiness and difficulty staying alert. To counteract sleepiness, it is essential to create a conducive environment for practice, such as sitting in an upright posture or engaging in mindful walking. Incorporating gentle movement, like stretching or deep breathing, can also help combat drowsiness.

Moreover, adjusting the timing of mindfulness practice to a time when you feel more awake and refreshed can be beneficial. By recognizing the signs of sleepiness and implementing these strategies, practitioners can overcome this challenge and sustain a focused and alert state of mindfulness.

Mindfulness in Everyday Life

Mindfulness is a transformative practice that integrates different parts of your daily life, work, and daily activities in one place. This unique skill offers practical tools to cultivate present-moment awareness, allowing you to engage fully in your tasks and interactions.

By applying mindfulness, you can unlock your creative potential and enhance your problem-solving abilities. It also enables you to approach challenges with clarity, openness, and curiosity, leading to innovative solutions.

Furthermore, mindfulness supports improved communication and relationships by fostering active listening, empathy, and compassion. By being fully present with others, you can deepen connections and build stronger bonds.

Moreover, mindfulness is a powerful tool for stress management and self-care. It helps to develop resilience and cope effectively with stressors, promoting overall well-being. By cultivating a mindful approach, you can create space for self-reflection, self-compassion, and self-care practices, fostering a balanced and fulfilling life.

The Integration of Mindfulness and Happiness

Mindfulness is "a state of cultivating non-judgmental awareness in the present moment, paying attention to thoughts, emotions, and bodily sensations without attachment or aversion." *Happiness*, on the other hand, encompasses "a state of subjective well-being and fulfillment." The integration of these two concepts explores the profound connection to how they enhance overall well-being and foster a deeper sense of happiness in individuals' lives (Crego et al., 2021).

By integrating mindfulness into our daily lives, we develop the ability to observe our thoughts and emotions with greater clarity and acceptance. This heightened self-awareness allows us to recognize negative patterns of thinking and behavior, enabling us to respond to life's challenges with more resilience and compassion. In addition, mindfulness cultivates an attitude of gratitude and appreciation for the present moment, fostering a deeper sense of joy and contentment.

Research suggests that mindfulness practices, such as meditation and mindful movement, can positively impact mental and physical health, reducing stress, anxiety, and depression. These practices promote emotional regulation and enhance overall psychological well-being, which are key components of happiness.

Furthermore, mindfulness encourages a shift from external sources of happiness, such as material possessions or achievements, to an internal state of well-being rooted in the present moment. By cultivating mindfulness, individuals can develop a greater capacity for genuine happiness that is not dependent on external circumstances.

In essence, the integration of mindfulness and happiness offers a powerful approach to living a more fulfilling and meaningful life. It empowers individuals to cultivate a deeper connection with themselves, others, and the world around them, ultimately fostering a profound sense of happiness and well-being.

Exercises

Exercise 1: Mindful Breathing

Meditation and calming down are among the basic techniques to practice mindfulness. Therefore, cultivating this habit into your daily routine can help you immensely to attain a positive attitude toward mindfulness and present-moment awareness.

All you have to do is to find a quiet and comfortable place to sit and focus. It could be your home, a park, or any other place you find comfort and peace.

Just sit and close your eyes and relax your body. Focus your attention on deep breathing. Notice your breathing patterns of air entering and leaving your body. If your mind wanders to negative thoughts, bring it back by focusing on breathing patterns again.

Practice this for 10 minutes daily and see what wonders this exercise does for you!

Exercise 2: Body Scan

The body scan exercise is a mindfulness practice that promotes relaxation and body awareness. This is a simple exercise that helps to reduce anxiety and calm your nerves.

Try lying down or sitting in a comfortable position. Bring your attention to different parts of your body, starting from the toes and moving up to the head. As you scan each body part, you observe any sensations, tension, or areas of discomfort without judgment.

By consciously breathing into those areas and intentionally relaxing them, you release tension and promote a sense of relaxation throughout your body. This exercise helps to calm the mind, increase present-moment awareness, and cultivate a deeper connection between the mind and body, fostering overall relaxation and well-being.

Exercise 3: Mindful Eating

This might feel far-fetched, but mindful eating can be a great way to indulge mindfulness in your daily life. Your eating patterns affect more than half of your behaviors, and one of them is mindfulness.

The exercise is to choose small meals such as raisins or small fruit slices rather than going for snacks when you feel hungry. This would help you avoid half of the junk you consume.

Also, try to take normal-sized meals. Don't indulge yourself in overeating. Take small bites and savor the flavors of your meals. Pay close attention to the chewing process and the act of swallowing, as these will help you engage all your senses and be more momentarily present.

Exercise 4: Daily Mindfulness Moments

Setting reminders throughout your day to pause and bring your awareness to the present moment is a mindfulness exercise that promotes relaxation and mental well-being.

When the reminder goes off, take a few deep breaths and tune in to your surroundings. Notice the sounds, smells, and sensations present in your environment. By consciously focusing on the present moment, you cultivate mindfulness and create a mental break from the busyness of your day.

This exercise allows you to anchor yourself in the present, reduce stress and anxiety, and develop a greater sense of calm and relaxation throughout your daily activities.

Chapter 5: Clean Out Your

Emotional & Physical Closet

Have you ever felt like carrying something heavy on your shoulders, weighing you down, and keeping you away from fully experiencing happiness? If so, you're not alone, my friend. We all have emotional baggage of unresolved conflicts, past traumas, and grudges that impact our well-being without us even realizing it.

Like an overstuffed suitcase, our emotional baggage holds negative experiences and unresolved emotions that make us unable to find true happiness. As long as we continue to carry the weight of these painful and unresolved memories, our journey toward genuine happiness and joy becomes a battle.

Here is the good news: We all hold the power to bring a change. By recognizing the importance of addressing and identifying our unresolved emotions, we can begin the process of cleaning out our emotional baggage. It's time to acknowledge them, lighten up the shadows of the past, and get the courage to face what you've been avoiding.

Let yourself free from the grip of unresolved conflicts or emotions of the past and create a space for healing, growth, and personal development that ultimately leads to authentic happiness.

Guess how you can do that? Setting the goal to clean out your emotional baggage is the first step toward a happier and more satisfying life. It's a commitment to your happiness and well-being—a conscious choice to face your emotional closet and get your happiness back.

Remember that this journey isn't going to be easy. It takes self-reflection, willingness, and vulnerability to face uncomfortable truths.

But the benefits are immeasurable. Such as you get an opportunity to heal, find inner peace, and reclaim your sense of joy. All In all, identifying your emotional baggage is crucial. Here's how you can acknowledge your emotional baggage.

Identifying Emotional Baggage

Emotional baggage often hides in the quiet corners of our hearts, making our lives harder and keeping us from being truly happy. Identifying our emotional baggage is an important step toward healing, personal growth, and lasting happiness. Past experiences and emotional traumas left imprints on our well-being, shaping us in profound ways. We need to acknowledge and understand the impact of these events to untangle the emotional knots of our lives that held us back.

Unresolved conflicts and grudges can create patterns that limit our true happiness. By bringing these patterns into consciousness, we learn more about the emotional baggage we carry. To get peace within ourselves, we need to address these patterns of unresolved conflicts and grudges.

When it comes to identifying emotional baggage, we must examine how negative self-talk and limited beliefs impact our lives. They erode our self-esteem and limit our actual potential. By examining these beliefs, we can challenge and revise them so that they are replaced by more empowering scripts. Practicing self-compassion and positive affirmations fosters personal development and emotional well-being.

In addition to these self-explorations, we also acknowledge the emotional weight of past relationships. Those connections leave marks on our hearts, and their influence follows us into the present.

By recognizing how these relationships have changed us, we face the unresolved feelings they have left behind. By being honest with ourselves and reflecting on ourselves, we give ourselves permission to feel, heal, and let go of what no longer serves us. This process creates a safe space within us, allowing us to build healthier relationships and welcome new beginnings.

The Healing Power of Forgiveness

Forgiveness is a deep and powerful force that can heal and set us free. It is a deeply personal and empowering journey that offers a variety of benefits for our general well-being. By recognizing the significant influence forgiveness can have on personal growth, we realize its power to free us from resentment and anger and nurture our relationships with compassion and empathy.

Self-compassion and the willingness to release negative feelings about oneself are the foundations of forgiveness. Self-forgiveness releases the burden of self-blaming and self-judgment and creates a space for growth, self-love, and a renewed sense of purpose.

Apart from forgiving oneself, forgiveness also invites us to cultivate kindness toward others and let go of the grudges we may have. Forgiving others isn't about forgetting their hurtful action; instead, it's a conscious choice to release the emotional burden and allow ourselves to heal. When we choose to forgive, we take back our power and open ourselves up to a world of emotional freedom, which brings us happiness.

Letting Go of Toxic Relationships

Letting go of toxic relationships is another important step toward positive emotional well-being. It's not easy to cut off some people from our lives who meant so much to us at some time. So, to let go of the relationships, the first step is to recognize their presence in our life. We need to develop an awareness of the patterns, dynamics, and behaviors of such relationships and how their negative impact is affecting our lives.

Then, we need to set boundaries! These boundaries help us to establish guidelines for acceptable behaviors and protect emotional health. Setting boundaries involves saying no to unhealthy patterns, asserting your needs, and detaching yourself from toxic influences.

After setting boundaries, the next step we need to do is to realize that some attachments that no longer serve us are good to be released. It liberates us from the chains of toxic attachments and opens the door to new opportunities and healthier connections.

As we let go of toxic attachments, it becomes essential to surround ourselves with positive and supportive people. People who inspire and uplift us provide a safe and empowering environment that helps us become more resilient and even happier.

Emotional Release Techniques

Several emotional release techniques help us to release our emotional baggage to lead us to healing, self-expression, and personal development. One of the powerful techniques is journaling. It helps us to channel our thoughts, feelings, and experiences onto a page, which allows us to process them in a safe and non-judgmental space. It provides an opportunity for self-awareness, self-discovery, and a deeper understanding of our emotions and feelings.

Another important technique is engaging ourselves in cathartic practices, like writing letters or practicing burning rituals. It helps us to release pent-up emotions. Writing letters to oneself or others to express our thoughts, grievances, or forgiveness can be profoundly therapeutic. Burning rituals help us shed emotional baggage by watching them convert to ashes.

On the other hand, seeking professional help, such as therapy or counseling, provides us with a structured and compassionate space for emotional release. It gives validation and acceptance to our emotions and feelings. It also helps us gain insight, process trauma, and develop healthy coping mechanisms to face new challenges in our lives.

Art therapy is another key technique, which allows us to express our emotions non-verbally. Other energy healing techniques, like Reiki or acupuncture, work on an energetic level to restore balance, clear emotional blockages, and enhance our general well-being.

Cultivating Emotional Resilience

Emotional resilience is a journey that changes us and gives us the power to handle everyday challenges with grace and strength. Developing the ability to recognize and control your emotions is a key part of building emotional resilience. The more we explore our feelings, the more in sync with our interior world we become. It helps us recognize our emotions and deal with them in constructive ways.

Self-care is a crucial component of nurturing our emotional well-being. When we put ourselves first, we take care of our physical, social, and emotional needs. This means doing things that make us happy, help us relax, and give us energy. Self-care rituals like practicing mindfulness, engaging in hobbies, or spending time in nature enhance our sense of inner peace and happiness.

Furthermore, building a supportive social network of trusted people helps to cultivate emotional resilience. Being surrounded by supportive people makes us empowered, resilient, and truly happy. Moreover, we need to embrace vulnerability and allow ourselves to be open and authentic to ourselves and others, which ultimately leads us to immense personal development and emotional resilience.

Creating Emotional Boundaries

First thing first, recognize and communicate your emotional needs to create emotional boundaries in your life. This allows you to maintain healthy relationships and prevent you from building up resentment or frustration.

Boundaries define limits and evaluate what is acceptable and respectful in your interaction with others. They protect your energy and emotional well-being by ensuring that your emotions, needs, and values are respected. They establish a balance between giving and receiving love from others.

Learn to say no, which includes knowing your limits and accepting commitments. Respecting your limits and refusing requests or situations that exceed your talents, prioritize self-care and prevent burnout. Saying no protects you and lets you focus on what matters.

In addition, emotional boundaries require assertiveness in expressing feelings and needs. Communicating openly, honestly, and politely promotes healthy communication, problem-solving, and understanding in relationships. Assertiveness gives you the power to own your feelings, stand up for yourself, and find a balance between asking for what you want and taking into account how others feel.

Embracing Emotional Growth and Healing

Emotional growth and healing require a lifelong commitment to self-discovery, self-reflection, and personal development. They involve recognizing that emotional growth is a continuous process rather than a goal that you want to achieve. Continuing self-reflection and exploring emotions are a foundation of emotional growth and healing. They give insight into our patterns and triggers and help us heal our emotional wounds.

Discovering fresh opportunities for personal development and growth is a crucial element in embracing emotional growth and healing. This transformative power includes attending workshops and therapy sessions or seeking guidance from experienced mentors or coaches.

Engage in activities that challenge us, such as learning new skills or pursuing hobbies. This expands our comfort zone and fosters personal growth. Moreover, these activities help us confront our fears, build resilience, and enhance our self-awareness.

Don't forget to acknowledge and appreciate the progress you make along the way, no matter how small it is. By celebrating your accomplishments, you'll reinforce the positive changes in yourself, which motivates you to continue to grow. Besides, it allows you to treat yourself with kindness, understanding, and forgiveness as you navigate the ups and downs of your emotional journey.

Declutter Your Space to Declutter Your Mind

Our physical environment plays a major role in our mental well-being. It is important to understand that our physical environment and mental well-being are connected. Our surroundings influence our emotions and moods, while our mental well-being shapes our perception of our surroundings.

Decluttering is highly beneficial for reducing stress and enhancing mental clarity. The practice of decluttering creates a more organized and visually appealing space, which reduces frustration and fosters a feeling of accomplishment.

In addition, decluttering decreases sensory overload, which makes the environment calmer and makes it easier to relax and/or to focus. It provides an opportunity for self-reflection and the release of emotional burdens.

The Impact of Clutter on the Mind

Start by understanding the impact of physical clutter on your mind. Cluttered spaces in our surroundings create a feeling of overwhelm, anxiety, and distractibility.

The presence of excessive belongings in our environment can overwhelm us mentally and visually, which makes it difficult to concentrate and find a sense of calm. When you recognize the negative influence of clutter on your mind, you become motivated and take action to declutter your spaces. A messy desk, messy house or messy room is akin to a messy mind, and keeps us from finding focus, relaxation or inner peace.

The Benefits of Decluttering

Decluttering your space isn't just tidying up; it also impacts your well-being effectively. Here are several benefits of decluttering:

- A clean and organized environment provides you with a sense of inner peace and relaxation.

- Visual order and cleanliness have psychological benefits that allow you to experience greater peace of mind.

- It reduces distractions and enhances productivity and focus, allowing you to concentrate on important tasks.

When you declutter, you make room for clarity and creativity and enhance your physical as well as emotional well-being.

The Decluttering Process

To begin the decluttering process, it's crucial to have a plan in place. Start by assessing the clutter and identify the problem in your space. Then, plan how you're going to declutter; specify areas or categories you want to tackle. Set realistic goals as it helps to stay focused and motivated throughout the process.

Once you've planned the process, it's time to sort and organize the belongings. Consider efficient decluttering techniques such as the *KonMari* method and the Four-Box Technique.

Classify objects and determine which to keep, donate, or discard. I understand that letting go of emotional attachments to sentimental objects can be difficult, but remembering is essential for decluttering. It depends on you how you overcome attachments and make sensible decisions. If it something you haven't used, worn or thought of in the last few weeks, it is probably not something you NEED to keep.

Minimalism and Its Benefits

Minimalism is a lifestyle that aligns with decluttering and can provide additional mental health benefits. Embrace the core principles of minimalism, such as intentional living, simplicity, and prioritizing what truly matters.

Minimalism promotes mindfulness, encouraging you to be more aware of your consumption habits and to avoid making unnecessary purchases. By adopting a minimalist mentality, you can increase your presence and contentment while decreasing mental clutter.

Cultivating a Clutter-Free Mindset

Decluttering your space is not a one-time thing; it requires you to shift your mindset and change the way you think. Practice *mindful consumerism* by making deliberate choices about buying new things.

Avoid unnecessary purchases that may contribute to future clutter by employing mindful shopping practices.

Establish regular maintenance and mindful habits to stop clutter from building up. Develop habits for getting rid of clutter and cleaning up, as they will keep your space organized and help you keep your mind clear.

Verdict on Decluttering

Decluttering your physical environment is an effective method for clearing your mind of clutter. You can appreciate the benefits of decluttering if you comprehend the impact of chaos on your mental health.

Create an environment that promotes relaxation, concentration, and mental clarity through cleanliness and order. Adopt a minimalist lifestyle to cultivate mindfulness and contentment. By cultivating a clutter-free mindset and sustaining your space regularly, you can achieve mental clarity and tranquility.

Key Takeaway

Now, reflect on how releasing emotional baggage impacts your life positively when you clean out your emotional closet. Remember, self-compassion and forgiveness are two crucial elements throughout your journey. Moreover, it's important to explore your emotions and take your first step toward healing. Celebrate your little milestones. Clean your emotional closet and declutter your physical space from time to time. Follow these steps and make your life happier and more fulfilling.

Exercises

Exercise 1: Journaling

Journaling is one of the most powerful practices that greatly contribute to our emotional well-being. Take some time, set aside in a calm place, and write down whatever you're feeling. It allows you to express your emotions and feelings in a safe and non-judgmental space. It also helps to let go of the grudges that you hold. It gives you insight into the emotions on your well-being, fosters a deeper understanding of self, and paves your way for healing and growth.

Exercise 2: Forgiveness Practice

Reflect on your relationships and identify if someone hurt you, and you need to forgive them, either yourself or any other person. Recall the pain or hurt that situation or person caused you. Then, write down your feelings on a piece of paper. Understand the circumstance and the person and forgive them. Release all the negative emotions and grudges that are connected with the situation. Forgiveness promotes healing and allows you to release the emotional load you've been carrying on your shoulders for so long.

Exercise 3: Surrounding Yourself With Positive Influences

A positive support system enhances your physical as well as emotional well-being. To surround yourself with positive influence, you need to evaluate your relationships. Identify the toxic or draining connections that you're holding on to. Set your boundaries and distance yourself from people who give you any kind of negative vibes. Then, look at you positive and supportive people who inspire and uplift you. Build relationships with people who share similar values and aspirations with you.

Exercise 4: Gratitude Practice

Gratitude brings joy and fulfillment into our lives. You can practice gratitude by writing a gratitude journal or creating a gratitude jar. You can write all the good things that happened to you throughout the day or express something you're grateful for. Reflect on the positive things that happen in your life and all the things you're blessed with. Gratitude practices foster a positive mindset and help to improve well-being.

Exercise 5: Cleaning Up Your Space—Declutter

Decluttering practice helps you to clean up your mind. Begin with choosing a space; it can be in your house, office, or car. Schedule your days for each place. Then, start with a small step, such as cleaning up a drawer. It gives you a sense of accomplishment and satisfaction. Now, it's time to make up a plan to reorganize and reduce the mess in your home and life.

Chapter 6: Self-Control and Life-Long Habits for Happiness

We might only think about how much self-control we have, when we are trying to resist eating something calorie rich, but it is all too important in controlling our reactions and emotions too. Our ability to control our feelings, and impulses are one of the main pillars of a positive and healthy lifestyle.

People often ask, "Can self-control lead you to happiness?" Of course! Being able to control your impulses and instincts will shift the outcomes of your situations into better ones, and this will surely make you happy.

Many people don't consider it important, but building and practicing fruitful habits make your mind a calm and happy one. Habits like kindness, gratitude, and empathy benefit you socially and mentally. Exercise is a makeshift way to release stress. And living along a steady routine makes you healthy. All these things lead to happiness in one way or the other.

By managing your reactions that cause you to impulse buy or lash out in anger, you can control yourself and the situation. Self-control, at times, gives you a clear picture of your surroundings and guides you to make better decisions. Also, imposing life-long habits that nurture you brings out a better version of you. This is a long-term assurance of well-being. By doing this, your happiness is certainly assured.

This chapter is here to give you all the tips on how to develop self-control and life-long nourishing habits for a happier life. So, let's get started together!

The Power of Self-Control

Self-control is a virtue by which you can become a whole new being. It is a trait that enables you to explore more about yourself. Your likes and dislikes, temptations, triggers, etc. Furthermore, self-control is a realization of rights and wrongs in you. By learning to control how you act in circumstances of different genres, you can manipulate the results to be in your favor.

What Is Self-Control?

To implement self-control in our lives, first, we need to understand what *self-control* really is. According to the American Psychological Association (APA), "It refers to the ability to regulate and restrain one's impulses, emotions, and behaviors" (*APA Dictionary of Psychology*, n.d.). It involves making deliberate choices and resisting immediate gratification or impulsive actions in favor of long-term goals or values, and is usually taught and mastered in adolescence.

Self-control allows us to manage our desires, maintain focus, and make rational decisions, ultimately leading to improved self-discipline and overall well-being.

However, it is a characteristic not possessed by many. I was personally taught self-control from a very young age, both my parents and my gymnastics coaches drilled into me self-control and instilled in me the ability to be self-disciplined and motivated. These three traits go hand in hand and our big pillars to accomplishing tasks and achieving what you want.

People who lack these skills often fall into the hands of their past actions and make their present and future suffer.

Self-Control—A Way to Achieving Goals

Self-control is a vital tool in achieving goals. It enables individuals to resist temptations, stay focused, and make disciplined choices. By exerting self-control, people can delay instant gratification for long-term rewards, overcoming distractions and obstacles along the way.

Developing self-control fosters discipline, resilience, and perseverance, empowering individuals to make rational decisions that align with their aspirations. With self-control as a guiding force, individuals can navigate challenges, stay on track, and ultimately achieve their desired outcomes.

This habit helps you to focus on your ambitions more clearly. It gives a boost and stimulates you to perform well. You become able to make a clear path to follow. As a result, your mind becomes sharp, and your achievements become profound.

Self-Control Strategies

Self-control plays a key role in living a satisfactory life. Because of your ability to manage yourself, you seek what you want, and as a result, you are happy. Keeping you away from stressful conditions and self-control undermines happiness in all aspects.

The following are some strategies that you may find helpful in cultivating a self-control attitude in your life:

1. Overcome your temptations.

Temptations are the front-line destroyers of your mental peace and physical health. According to a study performed in 2016 by the American Psychological Association, training to overcome temptations greatly helps in building self-control (E. Sheeran et al., 2016).

By recognizing and resisting immediate temptations, individuals can avoid impulsive actions that may derail their long-term goals. This involves practicing mindfulness, being aware of triggers, and developing strategies to counteract them.

Employing techniques like distraction, self-reflection, or reframing can help redirect attention away from temptations and strengthen self-control. If you feel like you are inconsistent with controlling these temptations, have a friend or a family member keep a check and balance on you. This trick helps a lot when it is difficult to manage them yourself.

By consistently resisting temptations, you can build resilience, strengthen your willpower, and foster greater self-discipline.

2. Develop a stress coping mechanism.

It is a known fact that self-controlling persons are better at coping with stress and difficult circumstances. A study was done by Kristian Steensen Nielsen on a total of 594 persons in the United Kingdom. This study revealed that people who practice self-control had more stable stress levels as compared to people with lower self-control levels (Steensen Nielsen, 2020).

Effective stress management tools can help you better regulate your emotions and impulses.

Engaging in activities like exercise, mindfulness, or journaling helps reduce stress levels and prevent impulsive behaviors triggered by stress.

Developing healthy coping mechanisms empowers individuals to handle stress in a constructive manner, enabling them to make more controlled decisions and maintain self-discipline in challenging situations.

3. Clarify your *why* to self-control.

By clearly understanding and defining the reasons behind your goals or desired behaviors, you create a strong sense of purpose and motivation. To improve self-control when facing immediate gratification, it's beneficial to pause and clarify your *why*.

Take a moment to reflect on your core motivators and jot them down in a journal or on a visible homemade sign. By keeping this list in your home or workspace, you'll be reminded of your goals and values, making it easier to resist temptation and make choices aligned with your long-term aspirations.

This clarity helps you stay focused, resist temptations, and make disciplined choices aligned with your values. When faced with challenges or distractions, reconnecting with your *why* can reinforce self-control and keep you on track toward achieving your objectives.

Putting a Full Stop to Unhealthy Habits

Unhealthy habits are "those habits that are unhelpful and lead us down the wrong path in life." These are some actions that you may be fond of knowingly or unknowingly. At times, they can lead to physical health problems, such as obesity or cardiovascular issues, and contribute to mental health issues like stress, anxiety, and depression.

Unhealthy habits, such as a sedentary lifestyle, poor diet, excessive alcohol consumption, or smoking, can be a major hurdle on your path to happiness. These activities reduce energy levels, impair cognitive function, and hinder productivity.

They can also strain relationships and limit overall life satisfaction. Breaking unhealthy habits and adopting positive behaviors are crucial for improving our well-being and achieving a healthier and more fulfilling life.

Triggers Behind Unhealthy Habits

Triggers for unhealthy habits can vary widely. They can be emotional, such as stress, boredom, or sadness, prompting unhealthy coping mechanisms. Social triggers, like peer pressure or societal norms, can also influence bad habits.

Environmental cues, such as proximity to certain substances or situations, may play a role. Additionally, habit loops, where a cue prompts a routine and rewards reinforce the behavior, can perpetuate bad habits. Understanding these triggers can help individuals identify, address, and control the underlying factors contributing to their unhealthy habits.

For example, if you are well aware that being tense leads you to nail biting, when you start to feel tense you can have the self-control now to reduce your nail biting by sitting on your hands, getting up and going for a walk or finding another way to reduce your tension level without needing to bite your nails.

Strategies to Control Unhealthy Habits

Setting yourself free from actions you have pursued for a long time is actually not as easy as it looks. It requires consistent efforts and hard work to break free from these bad habits. Considering the above example again, your habit of nail biting is triggered by being tense.

Here are some strategies that can help you stop repeating your bad habits

You can practice the following methods:

- Change the circumstances to create a clean slate

- Swap your bad habit with a new healthy one

- Monitor your bad habit

- Make your bad habit incredibly inconvenient

For many of us, the easiest time to implement better habits is when we are moving, starting a new job or having some kind of new beginning. When our slate of bad habits is quote on quote wiped clean and we are free to start a new lifestyle without the weight of all the bad ones, creating new and better habits is much easier.

Financial Well-Being via Minimalism

At the time of publication of this book the US is in a terrible recession, interest rates are high and the overall stability of our collective consciousness feels rocky. Many people have said money doesn't buy happiness but financial well-being certainly helps.

There are many reasons why people struggle with money. It may be due to different factors like being born into a mediocre family, unemployment, or overspending, and whatever the case may be, there are always solutions to save more and spend less. Stressing over incompetent finances leads you to major medical and non-medical conditions, thus disrupting your happiness.

Having expert control over your financial matters will assure you fewer encounters with money-related stressful situations. To avoid situations like this, try not to overspend during the initial days of the month; saving as much as possible for emergencies will be very helpful. This certainly isn't a book on finance, so if finances are a large part of your unhappiness, I recommend talking to someone you know that's great with money or hiring a financial planner to help you come up with a plan to reduce debt and increase savings.

One easy way to save money is to adopt a minimalist lifestyle which is more beneficial than being an over spender, minimizing means to simply avoid spending too much on unnecessary items.

Keep track of your budget now and then. Some minimalistic habits that can help you toward a happier lifestyle are:

- Go shop thrifting.

- Be economical.

- Eat less delivery food and cook at home.

- Practice the three R's—Reuse, Recycle, and Reduce.

- Reuse clothes.

Apart from this, you can adopt different methods and strategies to spend less. Try to make a budget planner and track down your earnings and spending. Also, save a little for the rainy days. Avoid impulse purchases and restrict yourself from spending too much on one specific thing. All these things automatically give you self-satisfaction and peace of mind.

Eating Habits and Self-Control

Controlling eating habits is far more important than you think and plays into our happiness in ways in which you may not yet understand. A big part of our interests and everyday events revolve around food. Eating is not only a way to express our emotions but a coping mechanism for emotions we are trying to suppress. Both overeating and eating the wrong things can have detrimental outcomes to our health, wellbeing and ultimately our happiness. Obesity, heart disease, diabetes and some cancers can all be provoked by eating an unhealthy diet, so changing these unhealthy habits is crucial to a long life.

What we eat can often be rooted in our upbringing, and our culture, but convenience and our income level also tie into the choices we make in purchasing food items. These factors can make changing our diet habits difficult, but nothing impossible when we have a plan and some self-control.

First and foremost when it comes to diet avoiding processed foods and items high in sugar are a must. An organic diet rich in fruits, vegetables, whole grains, healthy fats and protein are the best diets for overall health. Studies on the Blue Zones where people live the longest have also shown the Mediterranean diet, one rich in nuts, grains, healthy fats like olive oil, fish and vegetables are the best for longevity.

The best way to see if you are overeating is to keep a food journal, while also keeping track of how many calories you burn in any given day. If you are trying to lose weight you should be consuming less calories than you burn and to maintain your weight these should be close to even. And remember, portion sizes are just as important as the items you are putting into your body as well.

Whatever changes you decide to make, write them down, start small and stick to your plan. Exercise should be part of your everyday routine as well. Try to get in 60 minutes of moving time per day, especially if you spend a lot of time sitting. Most new habits take at least 21 days to stick, so challenge yourself to a 30 day healthy eating or exercise plan, to kickstart these new habits and routines.

Cultivating Life-Long Habits

Your lifestyle plays a great role in your happiness. Cultivating life-long habits fosters self-control for a happy life. A supportive daily routine and a positive environment help in building these habits.

By practicing consistency and discipline and embracing a growth mindset, individuals develop the ability to resist impulses, make intentional choices, and prioritize long-term well-being.

These habits empower people to lead fulfilling lives aligned with their values. This may seem like a difficult task to perform but is not. With a few positive amendments, your lifestyle will surely be an exemplary one. Here's how you can do this!

A Supportive Daily Routine

Conscious control and healthy management will have a positive effect on your daily routine. You can indulge in productive actions and tasks that will encourage your mind and favor your physical well-being as well.

Start with simple tasks like waking up early, making your bed and going to bed early. Adequate sleep is extremely important to our health as well and most American's certainly do not get enough. Aim to get 7 hours of sleep and avoid blue lights from phones and screens for the 30 minutes leading up to sleep and the first 30 minutes of your day after you have risen.

Our bodies and minds need rest, hydration and movement so each and every day these simple three things should always be priorities. I start every morning with a glass of water, some brisk exercise to get the blood moving and a few minutes of mindfulness in the form of meditation or yoga before getting on my phone or computer.

Creating a Conducive Environment

An environment that is parallel to your intentions of cultivating positive habits is what you need to build for a happy mindset. Being surrounded by an environment that does not match your intentions will be a mere temptation for you to turn back to your old ways. For instance if you are trying to avoid sugar you will not want to have cookies in your cupboard, and the same goes for any habit you are trying to change.

You need to create your space and design it in a way that motivates you to perform well and helps you self-regulate. Our inside spaces like our bedrooms, our offices and even our vehicles can be breeders of chaos and dysfunction. Creating clean, organized spaces provides for an organized and efficient mind and body. If you have a hard time focusing, look around your house, does it have the same dysfunction that you feel when you try to complete a task? Cleaning up our environments allows us to better focus on what we need to, as we are then less distracted by all that surrounds us.

Harnessing the Power of Consistency and Discipline

Discipline is "the ability to conduct one's actions in a manageable way" and *consistency* is "to keep it up." Both these traits are of impeccable importance in cultivating life-long habits that foster your way toward happiness.

Those lacking these traits stagger from their path and often leave their aims and intentions unattended. Harnessing the power of consistency and discipline ensures positive results in cultivating mindful habits.

Embracing a Growth and Self-Improvement Mindset

Too often we blame others for the disappointments or negative things that have happened to us in our lives. Instead of doing this you must embrace a mindset of growth, change and self-improvement. We are responsible for our own destinies, we alone have the power to make choices for ourselves. Blaming your parents, your spouse, or your boss for your own choices, failures or faults will do you nor anyone else any good. Instead, start believing that the things are happening for you, not to you. There are always different ways to view every situation. Open your mind to positivity and self-awareness so instead of finding anger or self-loathing you can find self-discovery and improvement. Just like businesses and governments have to evolve as times change so do we as individuals, there is always something to learn, and there is always someone in which you can improve.

Nurturing Self-Control in Relationships

Self-control in relationships promotes better understanding and builds a strong bond based on the elements of respect and integrity within both parties. It makes communication much better and makes you worthy of resolving conflicts.

By setting boundaries and practicing acts of empathy and emotional control, your relationships tend to go on for a longer period of time.

Being outrageous and unaware of your own impulses makes you suffer in relationships. You need to take effective control of yourself when interacting with people.

Self-Control Strategies to Follow in Relationships

Self-control in relationships is "a skill that confirms security and peace for you and your companions. It demands control over your actions and words in anger, making wise decisions, and feeling for others as well."

Some self-control strategies for a healthier relationship include:

- Emotional regulation: In relationships, there are countless times when your emotions may be heightened, especially in disagreements with your spouse or family members. Having self- control to walk away, take 5 or stay calm can mean the difference between an argument and a solution.

- Empathy and understanding: It helps to understand what others are going through. Try to place yourself in other people's situations to feel what they feel. By doing so, you can build a trustworthy relationship.

- Active listening: Listening to others' points of view without rushing to respond and allowing them to make a clear statement will strengthen your relationship.

- Setting boundaries: It is vital to set boundaries with a partner, and even more so it is important to respect your partners boundaries. Boundaries can both be mental, emotional, physical and task based. Make sure you express what yours are to your partner for success. Such relationships tend to be more sustainable and long-lived.

Apart from the above methods, try to cultivate positive and healthy habits within a relationship. The habits that secure communication, trust, honesty, and respect for each other. Try to indulge in healthy talks where you share thoughts and experiences that will nurture your relationship and lessen the chances of quarrels over trivial matters.

Sustaining Self-Control Through Self-Care

Engaging yourself in sustainable self-care activities has proved to lessen the risks of illness and stress and increase your physical energy. Taking measures to promote your healthy growth by focusing on yourself is an effective self-control protocol. Any action that reduces personal stress and excites productive waves to you is self-care, and there are ways big and small we can do this in our everyday lives.

Prioritizing self-relaxation and getting engaged in beneficial activities will surely keep you at rest. Moreover, having a sound sleep is one of the most effective methods to freshen up. Apart from that, meditation, journaling, gardening, or any kind of hobby or act that you enjoy doing and is preferred to rejuvenate your mind and body in your leisure time is also self-care.

Stress plays a significant role in disrupting self-control. This is so because it keeps your mind in low esteem and refrains you from focusing on yourself. Self-care imports positive energy into you and fills you with hope. It encourages you to embrace yourself. Some simple destressing remedies are:

- Indulge in more physical activity.

- Create self-limiting space.

- Reduce screen time.

- Socialize with compassionate people.

- Do something you enjoy.

Moreover, celebrating self-control efforts with self-compassion makes up for an acknowledged process that corrects imperfections without being harsh and brings out the best in us. With self-compassion, self-control becomes a fulfilling journey rather than a constant struggle. Showering yourself with appreciation and kindness now and then does no harm. Simple ways in which to invoke self-care can be as simple as lighting your favorite candle at your desk, taking a bubble bath or even just going for a walk.

Exercises

Exercise 1: Self-Awareness

Self-awareness is "the ability to manage your thoughts and conscience, keeping an insight of your internal values. It creates a better sense of one's emotions." Cultivating self-awareness is a fundamental aspect of personal growth.

Make the following notes in your reflection journal or on a piece of paper:

- What triggers you? Either towards anger, sadness or temptation? Write these down.

- Write down 2 different ways in which you could respond when a triggering event happens than what you tend to do now.

- What are two actionable things you can do now to reduce these triggering events or temptations from happening?

This exercise helps build conscious control in you and makes you respond in a better way.

Exercise 2: Habit Tracking

- Monitor your bad habits. Then, decide which habits need to be removed firsthand and create an actionable plan to change them.

- Generate a habit tracker that consciously shifts your attention and restrains you from indulging in old actions again and again.

- Make a list of good habits that you wish to have. Start with one and commit to doing it on weekly basis for at least 30 days.

- Then, slowly increase the frequency and try to carry them daily. Do this until they become a part of your daily routine.

This exercise produces a sense of accountability in you, makes you consistent, and grooms you into a better person.

Exercise 3: Implementing a Morning Routine

Formulate a morning routine that goes best with your work and social life. Early morning walks, meditation, exercise, or reading habits bring your body in motion. Try to have a consistent rise and bed time with these tasks built into your routine.

Starting your day with positive intentions gives you more power and energy throughout the day. By undergoing this exercise, you will remain free from work-driven burdens as well.

Exercise 4: Embracing a Growth Mindset

Embracing a growth mindset includes recognizing your potential and what you are capable of. It can be implemented by:

- Reflect: Write down all the skills you have built in your life, how are you awesome, and what skills do you still want to master.

- Seek out learning opportunities for self-development. These could be physical or mental. Learning new skills challenges our mind to keep growing.

- Develop your grit. Find something you are interested in and take at least 5 minutes in your day to improve your skill. Sticking with something long term, especially when it's a challenge, grows your grit and perseverance.

This exercise fosters resilience, willingness, and adaptability toward upcoming life challenges, leading to confirmed achievements. This fosters a positive outlook on life.

Chapter 7: It's All About Mindset

Our mindset contributes profoundly to shaping our life experiences and outcomes. Like many other things, it may have a positive or negative influence on how we think, feel, or interpret situations. A positive mindset adds to our personal growth and personality. Whereas a negative one imitates you and creates a sense of self-doubt and staggering thoughts. Recent studies have shown that the people that live the longest have adopted a positive mindset towards their lives and the world around them.

A growth mindset is one that enables you to learn from setbacks and failures. It makes you accept criticism and work on your failings, grooming you internally as well. It makes you believe that your capacity and adaptability can be boosted by positive recurrences.

You should tend to embrace the fact that forming new abilities or traits can happen with continuous efforts and practices. Cultivating a growth mindset will lead to personal development and overall well-being. By orienting learning and self-awareness into our lives and shifting our thoughts to think of failures as opportunities we create a growth mindset full of positivity.

Here's how you can replenish yourself with a growing mindset and relieve yourself from your own limiting thoughts.

The Impact of Mindset

As said above, our mindset determines how we perceive and respond to challenges, setbacks, and opportunities. Whether it's a growth mindset fueling progress or a fixed mindset hindering growth, understanding its power can unlock untapped potential, foster resilience, and pave the path to personal and professional success.

What Is the Role of Mindset in Our Life?

Our mindset plays a significant role in our lives as it is a leading figure in how we act in situations. The way we perceive and think about ourselves and others is rationally due to our mindset. Having a powerful healthy mind restricts us from developing emotions like jealousy and aggression. It is the key factor behind our behavior patterns and emotional well, and our mind needs just as much exercise as our physical bodies do to stay in tip top shape.

Our mindset, also plays a pivotal role in how our life events turn out. A good mind set better sets the stage for major happenings of our lives to go as planned and deliver satisfaction and overall appreciation. It makes you believe you can do better. But a limited mindset will hold you back and keep you from being able to deal with what life throws at you.

By choosing a set of positive mental characteristics in ourselves, we can guarantee our personal growth and make our way toward success. By deciding not to give up on failures and considering them as a staircase toward betterment rather than mere setbacks, we can assure ourselves of positive growth.

Cultivating a Positive Mindset

Having a positive mindset allows you to always consider new perspectives and see different points of view. An accepting mindset helps you navigate your way toward your goals through challenging situations.

The following are some easy-to-administer remedies to help you cultivate a positive mindset:

1. Practicing self-awareness and identifying negative thought patterns

"Being aware of your actions and how they are generated" is called *self-awareness*. Other than that, "having a clear ground for your likes and dislikes" is also self-awareness. "To know yourself best" is another way to put it.

On the other hand, blaming others, assuming your an undermined person, being unrealistic, and having a negative approach to ways of life are considered negative thought patterns.

By keeping track of your thoughts on how they occur or what causes these specific unrealistic thoughts, you can slowly override them. Being mindful and observing your own thoughts without passing judgment is one way to have self-control over your mindset. Challenging your negative thoughts with a set of positive ones can also do magic.

Remember that self-awareness to control negative thoughts is not a task but a process and takes time. By practicing it more frequently, you can gradually makeshift negative thoughts with positive ones.

2. Challenging and reframing negative thoughts into positive ones

Whenever you catch yourself engaging in a negative thought, try to hush it from your mind. This is not easy in the beginning and needs continuous efforts and consistency. Learning how to break negative thoughts and challenging their validity can help you believe in realistic situations.

Try to replace negative and harmful thoughts with more healthy and positive thinking. Being compassionate with yourself and others will help you monitor your thinking. Indulge yourself in healthy sessions with a group of positive people. Listen and accept feedback from others by understanding their perspectives about life and its subsiding matters. A whole new window of thought processes opens in front of you in this way.

Here are some questions you can ask yourself to reframe your thoughts into more positive ones:

- Are there other ways of looking at this situation?

- Is there a better explanation than the one in my mind?

- How would I react if someone told me that they think this way?

- What do others think of this same situation?

3. Gratitude and positive affirmation

Positive affirmation means "to state your beliefs and values." Practicing gratitude by reflecting on things you are grateful for or by simply appreciating nature and surroundings is a path to happiness itself.

Gratitude is a thankful emotion. Take time daily to thank others for what they are doing for you and how you are inspired by them. Self-gratitude and appreciation of your constant efforts to achieve a positive mindset are also helpful. You can do both of these in a journal. Sending thank you cards is also a great way to express gratitude.

Affirmations should be jotted down as statements that motivate you and create a sense of self-confidence in you. Making a journal and writing positive notes for your future self to read will make you more thankful. Realizing how much you suffered and grooming yourself into a person having a healthy mind will keep you on track.

Focusing on gratitude and positive affirmations is an ongoing thought process that nurtures your mind with positive control and consistency. It grants you optimistic control over different life matters.

4. Positive influence and supportive environment

By fostering positive influence to generate a healthy and supportive environment, you can cultivate a good mindset. Supportive figures at your side always tell you that you are capable of doing much better and that you should not lose hope.

A supportive environment helps plant good thoughts in you. It keeps you away from negativity and helps you focus on productive things around you. Avoid engaging in habits that can be toxic to you. Stay away from discrimination, taunts, bullies, etc.

The most handy ways to build a supportive environment are as follows:

- Surround yourself with other positive people.

- Reduce negative exposure, which often means cutting contact with friends or loved ones that do not see life in a positive matter.

- Practice positive self-influencing.

- Try effective and healthy communication.

- Have supportive physical and mental growth.

Overcoming Limiting Beliefs

To acknowledge the power of limiting and conservative beliefs, we need to recognize them. We should learn how they play a role in developing a mindset against our well-being and personal growth.

What Are Limiting Beliefs?

Limiting beliefs are "deeply ingrained thoughts or convictions that hold us back from achieving our full potential. They are often formed through negative experiences, societal conditioning, or self-doubt."

These beliefs create mental barriers that restrict our actions, choices, and aspirations. They can manifest as thoughts like, *I'm not good enough* or, *I'll never succeed.* For a healthy and happy mindset, it is important to let go of these thoughts and work toward a more positive mindset.

How to Let Go of Limiting Beliefs?

The first step in letting go of limiting beliefs is to identify what these beliefs are for you. To recognize these unhealthy beliefs, gather up what you aim to do and then slowly make a list of thoughts that stop you from doing so.

Thoughts like, *Why should I? I won't make it! It's of no use!* are the basis of our limiting beliefs. Challenge the validity of your unrefined beliefs by demanding evidence and questioning it. Stepping out of your comfort zone by taking baby steps toward a new belief and letting go of the old one is also a good way to reframe your beliefs.

As you are learning to cultivate a positive mindset, reframing your beliefs into empowering ones is an essential step. Strong positive beliefs are possibilities that tend to give you an upper hand in various situations.

Various techniques, like sharing your beliefs and thoughts with a mentor or therapist, can help rejuvenate them. By seeking support from your friends and family, you can find out about the positivity around you. Reframing your beliefs with a, *What if I really can do it?* is to step out and take measures to become open to yourself.

A further effort by realization through visualization and indulging yourself in positive talks is a quick method to let go of a conservative mindset and accept other ways of thinking. By taking a look around, you can feel the positivity and goodness in things.

Embracing Resilience and Optimism

Resilience and optimism are crucial components of a happy and healthy mindset. Resilience allows us to bounce back from adversity, setbacks, and challenges. It involves developing the ability to adapt, persevere, and find solutions in the face of obstacles. By cultivating resilience, we learn to view setbacks as temporary and solvable, which fosters a positive mindset.

Optimism, on the other hand, complements resilience by influencing our outlook on life. It involves maintaining a positive perspective, expecting favorable outcomes, and focusing on opportunities rather than dwelling on problems. It helps us maintain motivation, persistence, and a proactive attitude, even in difficult times.

These qualities contribute to a path toward happiness by influencing our thoughts, emotions, and actions. A strong and positive mindset allows us to approach life's ups and downs with a sense of confidence and hope. It enables us to view challenges as opportunities for growth, seek solutions rather than succumb to negativity, and maintain a sense of gratitude and joy.

Moreover, resilience and optimism help us develop healthier coping mechanisms, reduce stress levels, and build stronger relationships. They promote self-belief, self-compassion, and a greater sense of control over our lives. Ultimately, embracing resilience and optimism empowers us to navigate life's uncertainties, find meaning and fulfillment, and create a happier and more fulfilling existence.

Mindset and Goal Achievement

Our mindset significantly impacts our ability to set and achieve goals. Whether it's cultivating a growth mindset, embracing resilience, or harnessing motivation. Understanding the intricate connection between mindset and goal achievement is essential for unlocking our full potential and reaching new heights of success.

Why Mindset Matters in Goal Setting?

Mindset matters in goal setting because it shapes our beliefs, attitudes, and actions. A growth mindset fosters resilience, embraces challenges, and sees failures as opportunities for learning and growth. It fuels motivation, perseverance, and a belief in one's ability to improve.

In contrast, a fixed mindset limits potential by fearing failure and avoiding challenges. By cultivating a growth mindset, we approach goal setting with a positive outlook, a willingness to take risks, and the determination to overcome obstacles.

A mindset focused on growth and possibility opens doors to new opportunities, enhances creativity, and maximizes our chances of achieving our goals.

How to Develop a Strong Goal-Setting Mindset?

Cultivation of a goal-setting mindset is not merely a task but a slow process that needs continuous efforts. A mindset that supports effective goal-setting is built through smartness and positive self-talk. Embracing what you have achieved so far and having a clear map of things that still need to be achieved in your mind helps you define your goal.

Here are some strategies that can help you in doing so:

- Write down your GOALS

- Harness a growth mindset: Appreciate having a growth mindset instead of a fixed one. Seek productivity and goodness around you and build a growing mind that embraces the act of hard work to achieve goals.

- Visualize your success: By using clear mental imagery and focusing your attention on your set goal, you can visualize success and achievement. This can help you in creating a strong plan on how to accomplish your aims.

- Positive beliefs: Positive beliefs mean positive thoughts. By cultivating encouraging thoughts and beliefs and letting go of limiting beliefs, you can achieve your goals steadily.

- Positive self-talk: Making positive affirmations and rendering productive self-talk also enhances your achievement toward set goals.

- Make your goals easy: Break down your tasks into easier steps so that it makes your goals easy to achieve. Do not overwork yourself; it may tire you up and break your consistency.

Mindfulness and Mindset

Mindfulness is "a practice that allows us to attend to the present. It involves conscious observance of our thoughts, behaviors, and emotions. It is an act that keeps us aware of ourselves and our surroundings." By practicing mindfulness, you endure self-awareness. You get to know about your impulses, behavior patterns, and sentiments.

Mindset is "a state that refers to how we think and look at the world. Our mindset is the key that builds up our presumptions and perceptions on matters of different categories."

It is a state that can be influenced by our surroundings, and we can shape it into different kinds. A mindset can be growing and creative or repulsive and fixed. A creative and growing mindset is inspired by positivity. On the other hand, a fixed mindset is stuck on limiting beliefs.

The practice of mindfulness provides a framework for a strong and growing mindset. It makes us non-judgmental in observance and testifies to positive outcomes. By synchronizing mindfulness and a positive mindset, we can have a better understanding of our capabilities and potential and nurture them by being aware of the present situations. Together, they provide meaning, focus, and clarity to our goals and help us overcome hurdles efficiently.

The Power of Self-Talk

Let's begin with understanding the definition of self-talk and its significance.

What Is Self-Talking?

"Having communication with your inner self" is referred to as *self-talking*. It is a process that many indulge in without realizing it. Basically, it means "going through situations mentally and picturing them, discussing stuff with yourself."

Significance of Self-Talking

The power of inner dialogue with yourself influences your mindset profoundly. It is the key to how you think of yourself. By self-talking, you can either encourage or discourage yourself. You indulge in self-talk at various times of the day without knowing it. And it depicts how you see yourself.

It can be depressive and negative or affirmative and positive. Negative self-talk hinders your way to success and becomes a leading cause of your constant failures. Whereas positive self-talk encourages you to do better and adds to your overall well-being.

Self-talk patterns are bound to change depending on ongoing situations around you.

It's important to have self-control over your thoughts and emotions in the regulation of this mind game. You need to keep them parallel to your goals. Keeping them productive and in your favor is the main task.

Here are some methods by which you can keep them growth-oriented:

- Replace negative thoughts with positive affirmations.

- Find supportive influencers around you.

- Be aware of yourself and your surroundings.

- Have appreciation and compassion for yourself.

- Practice the act of thankfulness.

Exercises

Exercise 1: Positive Affirmations

Positive affirmations are "inspirational statements that encourage your well-being and make you more prone to changes that are in your favor." To build an affirmative mind, you should:

- Create a list of positive statements that motivate you toward building a strong mindset.

- Try to indulge in them regularly; this is to cope with negative thoughts and replace them.

- Empower yourself with positive and supportive influences.

This exercise helps you become productive. By increasing the frequency of positive affirmations, your mindset flourishes rapidly into a strong one.

Exercise 2: Practicing Gratitude

Gratitude is "an act of thankfulness. By appreciating the good aspects of your life and being grateful for their existence, you can have a beneficial effect on your overall well-being."

To do so, the following activity is very fruitful:

- Take three things each day that you are grateful for and think about what would happen if they did not exist. Be thankful for them and share them with others.

- Make a gratitude journal and jot down events, things, and people you are grateful for. Write about their importance in your life.

- Focus on the blessings that you have rather than those that you lack.

By practicing gratitude for small things of nature and life, you can cultivate a broad and growing mindset.

Exercise 3: Visualization and Goal-Setting

The practice of creating vivid mental images makes you—mentally—believe that you have already achieved set goals. Visualizing success and feeling it will make you want to achieve your goals. Set small tasks that make goal achieving easy.

What you can do is:

- Follow a clear path in order to set goals.

- Create a vision board or mental map that keeps a record of your achievements and aspirations.

- Make goals that are in alignment with you so that there are few and easy-to-tackle hindrances in your way toward achieving them.

- Be regular and keep track of your progress.

This exercise makes it easy to cultivate a positive mindset by keeping your focus and mind clear.

Exercise 4: Indulging in Positive Self-Talk

The power of positive self-talk lies in the fact that it creates motivation within yourself. Being positive about yourself creates a sense of character representation in you. It encourages and motivates you to attain a healthy mindset. You can practice positive self-talk by:

- identifying negative thoughts and replacing them with productive ones

- paying attention to your thought patterns and indulging in a healthy dialogue with yourself

- being affirmative and kind to yourself

- creating mental support for yourself that helps you when you feel low

Embracing yourself through positive self-talk will contribute toward a growth-oriented mindset.

Chapter 8: Move Your Body and Breathe Fresh Air

In this uplifting chapter, we will explore the incredible power of embracing the joys of fresh air and physical exercise for our well-being. Furthermore, we will highlight the importance of setting a powerful intention to cultivate a life filled with vibrant health and wellness. Let's embark on a delightful journey as we explore each point in detail, uncovering the secrets to everlasting happiness.

We all are in search of finding our true selves. We will move toward self-discovery if we understand how much our happiness and success rely on our physical and mental well-being.

Through the words of this chapter, we will uncover the profound impact that taking care of ourselves has on every facet of our lives, from our relationships to our productivity. Nature therapy is a growing field all over the world, and I can concur that no matter how bad a day I am having, a few minutes spent in nature, listening to birds, feeling the sun, rain or wind on my skin and breathing in fresh air, instantly boosts my serotonin and leaves me feeling lighter, happier and more clear in my thoughts and emotions.

Furthermore, you will discover the invigorating effects of fresh air on your mind, body, and soul. Learn how spending time outdoors can rejuvenate your spirit, boost your energy levels, and enhance your well-being. Fresh air is a delightful gift that fills our lungs with life-giving oxygen, fueling our bodies to thrive and flourish.

Putting Your Hormones in Action

Meanwhile, physical exercise releases plenty of endorphins, the delightful *feel-good* hormones that elevate our mood, reduce stress, and improve our well-being. Engaging in regular physical exercise is a wonderful way to nurture our bodies. It has the incredible power to strengthen our cardiovascular system, enhance our immune function, and uplift our energy levels. By embracing this joyful practice, we start a journey toward a healthier and happier life.

Intention Is the Key

Intention is a magical key that unlocks our potential for happiness and fulfillment. It guides our gaze toward the bright possibilities and shapes our steps toward a joyful life. When we embrace this beautiful intention, we celebrate self-care and recognize the significance of nurturing our physical and psychological well-being. Now, we will see what steps ensure a happier and healthier life.

Fresh Air and Physical Exercise: Gateways to Happiness

Let's dig into the incredible benefits of fresh air and physical exercise and how they can transform your life into one filled with happiness and balance. Prepare yourself to go on a journey of self-discovery and well-being.

The Power of Fresh Air

Immersing ourselves in the embrace of nature's beauty and inhaling the invigorating freshness of the air has an extraordinary impact on our happiness and sense of well-being. Nature breathes new life into our souls, lifting our spirits and infusing us with boundless joy. The crisp, pure air revitalizes our bodies, nourishing them with oxygen and fostering a healthy respiratory system that enhances our immune system. Moreover, nature bestows a newfound clarity upon the mind.

For me, nature has always been the best place to think, to find peace, clarity, and a more intense connection with myself. There is something about the crisp, pure air that revitalizes our soul, nourishes our body with oxygen, enriches our cells with Vitamin D, and fosters health and happiness in our immune system.

Path to Finding Mental Clarity

Fresh air, like a gentle breeze with its calming effect on our nervous system, has the power to reduce stress, ease anxiety, and induce a state of blissful relaxation. How amazing!

Engaging in outdoor activities like hiking, gardening, or practicing yoga in nature breathes new life into our connection with the natural world, filling our hearts with pure happiness.

In the upcoming sections of this chapter, we will delve into the invigorating significance of physical exercise and its refreshing influence on our happiness.

Physical Exercise for Optimal Health

The impact of physical exercise on happiness cannot be overstated. It serves as a fundamental pillar for achieving optimal health, nurturing not only our physical but also our mental well-being. Research states that physical activity has been proven to improve the satisfaction of life and happiness in all age groups (An et al., 2020).

Your Physical Health Matters

Regular physical exercise has a profound impact on enhancing happiness by promoting a healthy body and mind. Participating in physical exercise not only boosts our happiness levels but also strengthens our muscles and improves cardiovascular health. Engaging in regular physical exercise has been found to decrease the likelihood of developing chronic diseases, including heart disease, diabetes, and specific forms of cancer.

Accelerate Your Mental Peace

Including physical exercise in your routine has a significant influence on your happiness and emotional state. Physical exercise has a remarkable impact on happiness as it triggers the release of endorphins, known as *feel-good* hormones. These endorphins work wonders by boosting mood, diminishing stress, and alleviating symptoms of anxiety and depression.

Ways to Achieve Happiness

- Physical activity outdoors has been proven to promote health and longevity when done consistently and reduce the onset of many diseases.

- Additionally, engaging in regular exercise increases energy levels, providing individuals with the vitality and motivation to tackle their daily activities with enthusiasm.

- Exercise plays a crucial role in fostering a positive body image and self-esteem, as it helps individuals feel more confident and satisfied with their physical appearance.

Focus on Your Personal Preferences

Engaging in physical exercise offers a multitude of options that cater to individuals' preferences and interests, thereby impacting happiness.

1. Cardiovascular exercises

Performing cardiovascular exercises such as running, cycling, or swimming can have a positive effect on happiness by elevating the heart rate and boosting endurance.

2. Strength training

Engaging in strength training exercises, whether it be lifting weights or bodyweight exercises, can lead to happiness.

3. Yoga or meditation activities

Physical exercises that improve flexibility and balance, such as yoga, Pilates, or tai chi, can have a profound impact on happiness and well-being. Engaging in these practices enhances posture, expands the range of movement, and fosters a sense of deep relaxation.

Steps to Perform Physical Exercise

The following steps can help improve happiness in your life through prioritizing physical exercise:

- Make a routine and follow it.

Developing a consistent exercise routine and setting achievable fitness goals are necessary to promote happiness in our lives. Dedicating time to exercise and committing to regular physical activity lead to a joyful life. Consistency is key in boosting happiness, as physical exercise has a profound impact on strength, endurance, and fitness levels.

- Set realistic fitness goals.

Setting achievable fitness goals is a crucial element that impacts the happiness derived from physical exercise. By engaging in regular physical exercise, you can break down large goals into smaller, attainable milestones, allowing you to track your progress and celebrate achievements along the way.

Engaging in regular physical exercise not only helps to maintain motivation but also fosters a profound sense of accomplishment, contributing to enhanced happiness.

It is a known fact that an active lifestyle makes things easier in the long run as you grow up, be it physical or psychological in nature. Let's find out how!

Creating an Active Lifestyle

Incorporating movement into our daily activities is a great way to cultivate an active lifestyle, which leads to happiness.

Choose Healthy Alternatives

Opting for healthy alternatives also matters! Choosing to take the stairs instead of the lift or walking or cycling for short-distance commutes leads to increased activity levels and promotes a more active lifestyle, which in turn contributes to happiness. These small changes can accumulate over time to make a difference.

There, as of now, is extensive evidence through research that staying active connects to mental well-being. For instance, epidemiological studies have shown that sedentary people are more likely to suffer from depression and anxiety than active people (Reynolds, 2016).

Advantages of Maintaining an Active Lifestyle

Exploring different forms of physical exercise is crucial for maintaining an active lifestyle, which leads to happiness. The following are some benefits of an active lifestyle:

- Cardiovascular exercises such as running, swimming, or cycling help elevate our heart rate, enhance endurance, and promote cardiovascular health, leading to increased happiness.

- Engaging in strength training exercises, like weightlifting or bodyweight exercises, contributes to the development of muscle strength and enhances bone health.

- Flexibility exercises, such as yoga or stretching routines, improve joint mobility and reduce the risk of injury.

The Power of Walking: Achieving 10,000 Steps Each Day

Walking is a simple yet powerful form of exercise that offers many benefits for our physical and mental well-being. By understanding these benefits, we can appreciate the unmatched power of walking.

Pros of Walking

- Walking improves cardiovascular health, aids in maintaining a healthy weight, and reduces the risk of chronic diseases.

- It boosts metabolism, strengthens bones and muscles, and improves fitness.

- Beyond the physical benefits, walking also has a positive impact on mental health by reducing stress, enhancing mood, and promoting relaxation.

Make Walking a Habit of Life

To make walking a consistent part of our lives, it's important to incorporate it into our daily routines. Instead of relying on scheduled workout sessions, we can find opportunities to walk in our everyday activities.

This can involve walking or cycling for short distances, taking walks during breaks, or exploring scenic routes on weekends.

Nature is beautiful, so do not waste any other second to implore its beauty! By integrating walking into our daily lives, we can accumulate steps and make it a sustainable habit.

Incorporating Mindfulness Techniques

Walking provides an opportunity to incorporate mindfulness techniques and enhance the experience.

Mindfulness Techniques

The following are some mindfulness exercises that you can incorporate into your life, especially when walking and accomplishing the 10,000 step-goal! Here are a few illustrations (Mayo Clinic Staff, 2020):

- Stay attentive.

- Be present right now.

- Show acceptance of self.

- Pay attention to your breathing.

Offering Strategies to Stay Motivated

Staying motivated is crucial in maintaining a walking routine. The following strategies can be helpful to keep your goal in mind and feel the motivation to achieve it:

- One effective strategy is to set milestones or goals to strive for. This can include increasing the number of steps taken each day or achieving specific milestones, such as walking a certain distance or completing a walking challenge.

- Tracking progress, either through a pedometer, fitness app, or journal, provides a visual representation of our achievements and keeps us accountable.

- Additionally, rewarding oneself for reaching milestones or walking can provide further motivation and reinforce the positive habit of walking.

How can we miss out on the incredible connection between our mind and body while talking about happiness? Let's dive into the understanding of this beautiful bond.

Mind-Body Connection

We all must embrace the harmonious connection between our mind and body. The beautiful symphony of the mind and body intertwines as their energies flow and merge, creating a profound impact on our well-being.

Recognizing the profound link between mind and body is crucial for cultivating a state of blissful harmony. When we nurture the intimate bond between our mind and body, we unlock the harmonious flow of happiness within us.

Get Ready for a Glow Up

By placing importance on our physical well-being, we invite a radiant glow of positivity to envelop our mental state.

Engaging in regular physical activity, consuming nourishing and wholesome food, and embracing restorative rest all contribute to the well-being of our mental state.

These practices not only reduce the burdens of stress but also uplift our spirits, fostering a positive and joyful mood.

Cultivating Mindfulness and Self-Care

Through the gentle art of mindfulness and the sacred act of self-care, we cultivate a deep sense of happiness that radiates from within. As we embrace these practices, we invite relaxation to permeate our being, soothing our bodies and minds.

In this tranquil state, inflammation fades away, allowing our bodies to heal and rejuvenate. Moreover, our immune system fortifies, standing strong and resilient against the challenges that may come our way.

The mind-body connection intertwines with happiness, creating a tapestry of wellness that nourishes every aspect of our being.

Art of Stress Reduction

The profound effects of exercise on our mental health are truly remarkable. When we take part in physical activity, our mind and body unite in a beautiful dance, igniting the release of happy hormones.

Let Your Happy Hormones Take Control

These incredible hormones flow through our being, spreading joy and nurturing a sense of happiness and well-being. Engaging in regular exercise harmonizes the intricate connection between mind and body.

It alleviates the burdens of anxiety and depression, allowing the spirit to soar. With each movement, self-esteem blossoms, radiating from within. The holistic benefits of exercise intertwine, nurturing the delicate tapestry of mental well-being.

Benefits of Exercise on the Mind and Body

The following are some benefits of exercising on the mind and body:

- Exercise serves as a harmonious bridge between the mind and body, intertwining the realms of stress relief and happiness.

- It diminishes the presence of stress hormones, like cortisol, while encouraging the emergence of mood-enhancing neurotransmitters, such as serotonin.

- Moreover, engaging in physical activity fosters a harmonious connection between the mind and body, promoting a sense of happiness and well-being.

- The enhanced blood flow to the brain not only nourishes brain function but also enhances memory and concentration, further enhancing the blissful state of being.

The role of the brain and its related functions cannot be denied. So, let's discuss how the brain needs exercise too, and explore the ways to perform these ahead.

Exercising Our Brains

As engaging in physical exercise is essential for our physical well-being, mental exercise is important for maintaining cognitive health and well-being.

Significance of Exercising Our Brains

The initial step in fostering our brains is acknowledging the significance of this. Engaging in mental exercise entails participating in activities that challenge and stimulate our minds, enhancing our memory, cognitive function, and problem-solving skills. Through the active engagement of our minds, we can take our mental abilities to another level.

Ways to Stimulate the Mind

The following are ways to exercise our minds and maintain their sharpness:

- learn or sharpen a new or developing skill. Challenging our brains is a great way keep them active.

- engaging in activities such as playing a musical instrument, acquiring a new language, or exploring a new hobby

- participating in puzzles, brainteasers, and brain games additionally offers a workout for the mind

- seeking novel adventures, like embarking on journeys, delving into uncharted territories, or immersing ourselves in diverse cultures

The new experiences and power of learning should be understood to cultivate happiness. So, let's find out how these experiences shape us.

The Power of Learning and New Experiences

Cultivating a growth mindset and possessing an insatiable desire for knowledge are crucial dispositions when it comes to engaging in mental exercises.

Importance of Learning

- Learning promotes adaptability, as we get new skills and perspectives that enable us to navigate different situations and challenges with ease.

- The act of learning cultivates a sense of curiosity and wonder within us, encouraging us to explore and discover new ideas, concepts, and possibilities.

- Through the act of embracing a mindset focused on lifelong learning, we can gain valuable insights and knowledge from our experiences. This approach allows us to grow and develop as individuals, uncovering new aspects of ourselves and exploring our passions.

- By remaining open to learning throughout our lives, we create a pathway toward personal growth and self-discovery.

Curiosity Is Not Bad

Encouraging curiosity and exploration of new subjects and interests is essential for fostering a love of learning. Curiosity acts as a powerful motivator, propelling us to seek out new knowledge and experiences. It fuels our desire for knowledge and stimulates our intellectual growth.

Experiences Are the Best Teacher

Embarking on a quest for new experiences allows us to embark on a life-changing journey. Through these experiences, we have the opportunity to expand our perspectives, nurture personal growth, and improve our well-being. By embarking on journeys to unfamiliar destinations and engaging with various cultures, we gain invaluable insights into a multitude of lifestyles, beliefs, and values. These experiences also contribute to our personal growth and help us become more self-aware.

Now, we will learn how we can balance our physical and mental abilities through exercising.

Balancing Physical and Mental Exercise

The art of achieving equilibrium between physical and mental exercise is a pursuit worthy of our attention. As we engage in physical activities to strengthen our bodies, it is important to engage in mental exercises to fortify our minds. By striking a harmonious balance between the two, we can unlock our full potential. How amazing does it sound?

By acknowledging the significance of incorporating both mental and physical exercise into our routines, we can cater to our holistic well-being requirements.

Nurturing Self-Care Through Health and Wellness

Taking care of your health and well-being are essential components of looking after yourself. Self-care goes beyond indulging in activities and includes taking care of our physical and mental well-being.

Take Out Time for Self-Care

Self-care is important to dedicate time and energy to both physical exercise and mental stimulation. Taking part in regular physical exercise is a wonderful way to care for our bodies, as it provides nourishment, enhances vitality, and uplifts our mood.

Activities to Promote Self-Care

Engaging in activities such as reading, learning new skills, indulging in creative pursuits, or practicing mindfulness can be great forms of self-care.

Creating a Self-Care Plan

By creating a thoughtful plan that incorporates activities for both our physical and mental well-being, we establish a holistic approach to taking care of ourselves. It is crucial to create a comprehensive self-care plan that considers your unique preferences, aspirations, and the importance of finding equilibrium in your life.

Steps to Create a Self-Care Plan

The following are the necessary steps to form a self-care plan:

1. Look at your routine.

Before coming up with a self-care plan, look at your current routines. What methodologies do you use to manage your life?

2. Recognize your self-care necessities.

Contemplate what you esteem most in your everyday life. Make a rundown of all your physical, mental, close-to-home, and expert necessities. A genuine illustration of taking care of oneself is one that thinks about all areas of prosperity.

3. Make a list of practices that meet your needs.

Now is the time to choose activities for self-care that will help you meet your needs. Consider asking yourself questions like:

- What exercises give me pleasure?

- What assists me with feeling energized?

- When do I calm down?

4. Fit them into your schedule.

This is the difficult part. To carry out these practices, you will need to find breaks in your hectic day. Keep in mind that taking care of oneself isn't childish. It's a thoughtful gesture to yourself.

5. Remove any obstacles.

Recall the negative propensities you distinguished before. It's time to let go of them. Start by lessening and afterward eliminating hurtful adapting propensities. Pick the most inconvenient one and supplant it with taking care of oneself and practice all things considered.

Remember. Integrating movement and fresh air into our lives is a personal journey. It requires consistency, self-compassion, and a willingness to explore and adapt.

By embracing the steps outlined in this chapter, we embark on a path of self-discovery and well-being, enhancing our lives and experiencing the true joy and fulfillment that happiness brings.

Exercises

Exercise 1: Regular Exercise

Get at least 30 minutes of physical activity daily. Do things like walking, dancing, yoga, or cycling that you look forward to doing. Incorporate exercise into your daily life and make it a top priority. This has positive effects on your physical health, mental state, and vitality.

Exercise 2: Going on an Outdoor Walk

Get outside and enjoy nature on a regular stroll in the woods, along the beach, or at a park. Use your senses to make a personal connection with the outdoors. Focus your attention on the present moment by taking in the peaceful sights and sounds of nature. You can get some exercise and enjoy the health benefits of being outside in the fresh air, but you can also unwind your mind and feel more in one with nature by doing this.

Exercise 3: Deep Breathing

Locate a peaceful and cozy spot to engage in some deep breathing exercises. Breathe in through your nose for a few seconds and out through your mouth. Keep your attention on the rising and falling of your chest as you inhale and exhale. Relaxation, stress relief, and enhanced concentration are some of the benefits of practicing deep breathing. This simple practice may be done almost anywhere, and it has a soothing impact almost immediately.

Exercise 4: Mindful Movement

Yoga and tai chi are only two examples of mindful movement practices that can be incorporated into daily life. As you go through each exercise, focus on how it feels in your body. Take several deep breaths and pay attention to the present moment while you're doing it. Physical health, mental serenity, and mental suppleness are all boosted by practicing mindfulness while moving.

Exercise 5: Knowledge Is Power

Make a point of expanding your knowledge every day. Use that time to read a chapter of a book, learn a new skill, or take part in a new hobby. This kind of mental activity keeps you from getting bored, piques your interest, and helps you learn new things. Adopting a mindset of perpetual inquiry fosters development and keeps the mind active.

Chapter 9: Spreading Kindness and Cultivating Meaningful Connections

Kindness is a wonderful way to create happiness. You might wonder how being kind to others can make you happy. The truth is human beings are simple creatures. Think of all the times you were upset. But a simple smile or greeting from a stranger on the subway has been enough to lift your spirits. You don't need big gestures to become happy. Deep down, you yearn for empathy, genuine care, and a sense of belongingness. These are the little things that will make you happy.

The Power of Kindness

Kindness has a massive impact on the personal well-being and happiness of a person. Performing acts of kindness improves happiness and life satisfaction among individuals. Kind people are more happy with their lives than the ones who do not express love and care for others (Rowland & Curry, 2018).

Exploring the Impact of Kindness on Personal Well-Being and Happiness

The interesting thing about kindness is that it is contagious. It has such a powerful force that it can transform you and those around you. Your kindness is going to start a chain reaction of warmth and love.

This ripple effect can help you discover your inner strength as a healer. It also has a dramatic effect on your relationships. All those conflicts and pain can go away in mere seconds with one moment of care and understanding.

Acts of Kindness

Kindness and care have the power to heal your trauma and sorrows. You think nothing in the world can help you now, but kindness has the power to heal your pain. This journey is hard; however, when you share and help others, you get closer to happiness.

Random Acts of Kindness

People always remember how you made them feel, and kindness makes them feel special. Hold the door open for someone. Compliment the dress of your fellow commuter. People love it when you notice these minor details about them. It makes them feel like the center of the universe and being the giver of this will also make you feel good.

Intentional Acts of Kindness

Did you ever think that something as easy as a smile can make someone happy? We all are looking for a moment of relief in this hectic life. A small smile from your barista, a stranger offering you an umbrella, or cuddles from your dog can make you happy. These little gestures require no effort, but their impact is huge.

You can also practice acts of kindness by making a to-do list of your intentional kind deeds. Every day, you are going to write down one simple and easy intentional act of kindness on your to-do list. It can be something as small as helping your housemate with the dishes, picking up trash on your street or volunteering at a charity. This way, you can practice kindness and play your part in society.

Cultivating Empathy and Compassion

Cultivating empathy and compassion is a lifelong journey. It requires you to be mindful of your own thoughts and feelings, as well as the thoughts and feelings of others. The first step is to listen with an open heart and try to understand others' perspectives.

Developing Empathy

As said, *"You never really understand a person until you consider things from his point of view. Until you climb inside of his skin and walk around in it"* (Lee, 1960).

This is empathy, the ability to understand and share others' emotions and feelings. Most of the time, you feel alone in this world. Although you have loved ones around you, you feel the absence of warmth in your relationships. This happens because you cannot tune in to the emotions of others. Sorrow is halved when shared, but sharing and understanding that sorrow isn't easy.

A key to being kind to people is to develop empathy. You should understand the feelings of your loved ones to help them. The better you are at understanding them, the kinder you are. Here are some exercises you can do to develop empathy.

- Empathy mapping: You can use empathy mapping as a visual tool to understand others. Create a diagram with four quadrants: Say, Do, Think, and Feel. Your diagram might look like this.

Say	Do
Think	Feel

Now, fill in the quadrants based on what you think the other person might say, do, think, and feel in a given situation. This exercise helps you gain a deeper understanding of others' emotions.

- Perspective-taking: Put yourself in someone else's shoes to understand their feelings and thoughts. Imagine how they will feel in a situation based on their background, experiences, and beliefs.

Practicing Compassion

Compassion is a powerful emotion that can have a positive impact on both the giver and the receiver. Cultivate a more compassionate mindset by indulging in mindfulness and active listening. Being grateful for your life can also help you become more compassionate and kind.

Showing compassion for yourself is as important as being compassionate to others. When you are kind to yourself, you are more likely to be happy and healthy. You are also more likely to be resilient in the face of challenges. Note that you can be kind to your body and soul by practicing self-care, eating your favorite foods, or cooking.

After you indulge in self-compassion, it is time to help others. You can do small acts of kindness for others, such as offering them a cup of tea or listening to them. Share their pain and listen to what they have to say.

Building Meaningful Connections

Building meaningful connections is the main thing you can do to create happiness. It can help you feel supported, loved, and understood. It can also help you grow and learn. There are many ways to build meaningful connections. Spend time with loved ones, volunteer, or strike up conversations with people you meet. When you build meaningful and genuine connections, you fulfill your need for belongingness (McLeod, 2023).

Nurturing Relationships

Nurturing your relationships is the product of authentic connections. These connections are essential for your well-being. They provide you with a sense of belonging, support, and love. In addition, they help you feel connected to something larger than yourself. Authentic connections are devoid of feelings of selfishness.

These relationships are born from care and warmth. Their purpose is to spread kindness in the community and your interpersonal relationships. You also achieve success in your professional life with the help of meaningful connections. Here are some tips for building and maintaining meaningful relationships:

- Practice empathy and compassion.

- Engage in honest and open communication.

- Spend time with others and do their favorite activities with them.

- Learn their likes and dislikes.

- Set healthy boundaries.

Active Listening

Active listening is a valuable technique used in therapy. It aims to convey sincere respect to another person. It involves attending to the speaker and being mindful of their emotions. Furthermore, empathy is an integral part of active listening.

Active listening is not only used in therapy. It is also a great way to convey respect and compassion in everyday conversations. It fosters a deep and meaningful connection.

- Make eye contact with the speaker.

- Lean in slightly to show that you are paying attention.

- Nod your head to show that you are listening.

- Paraphrase what the speaker says to show that you understand them.

- Ask clarifying questions to show that you are interested in what they have to say.

- Avoid interrupting the speaker.

- Be patient and allow the speaker to finish speaking.

Creating a Supportive Network

Seek out and surround yourself with positive and uplifting individuals. These people will help you to stay motivated and focused on your goals. Moreover, they will provide you with support and encouragement when you need it most. Positive people can have a profound impact on your life. They can help you see the good in the world, even when things are tough.

You can explore ways to build a supportive network. Begin by engaging in community activities, which are great to meet new people. You can find something that interests you and fits your schedule. Volunteer and outreach programs, support groups, and mentoring are great ways to get started.

Volunteering and Giving Back

Volunteering is a part of giving back to your community. It helps you create the ripple effect of kindness and compassion.

The Benefits of Volunteering

Volunteering has many interpersonal and intrapersonal benefits. It reduces your stress levels, improves mental health, and increases social connections. In addition, it can increase your self-esteem and feelings of well-being.

Volunteering gives you a sense of purpose. It is an opportunity for you to make a difference in the lives of others. It connects you with a cause that you care about. Volunteering is also a great way to develop empathy and practice compassion. You can find opportunities to volunteer in your local community or online.

Supporting Causes

Identify causes that align with your personal values and interests. You can do so by reflecting on what is important to you and what you want to change in the world. Look for causes related to your hobbies, interests, or profession. You need to learn more about your cause after you identify it. Research online or talk to organizations who work for similar causes.

The next step is to connect with organizations working on the causes you care about. There are several ways to lend a hand to your cause. You can donate money, take part in fundraising, or begin advocacy. Here are some things you should keep in mind before you begin:

- Choose a reputable organization to donate money.

- Set realistic goals for fundraising. Create a plan for how you will reach them and implement that plan.

- Gather research-related facts about your cause before you begin advocacy.

Spreading Kindness in Everyday Life

Do you want to become eternally happy? Well, I have the secret ingredient for you; kindness. Kindness will help you become the happiest person on earth. From your office to your house, everything will be transformed with small little moments of love.

Acts of Kindness in the Workplace

There are several ways to encourage kindness and positivity in professional environments. Give positive feedback and compliments to your colleagues. You can create a culture of appreciation in the workplace to boost morale and motivation. If your office has a hectic routine, take frequent but small breaks.

Prepare a cup of coffee for your workaholic office friend. Celebrate important milestones of their lives. These practices increase compassion in the professional environment. Kindness can also help build meaningful connections, and these are vital for a long and happy life.

Kindness in the Digital Age

The importance of spreading kindness in online interactions cannot be overstated. The internet can be a breeding ground for negativity. You must remember that there are real people on the other side of the screen, and your words have a real impact on them. Leaving a nice comment on someone's Instagram post will brighten up their day but a harsh comment can bring pain to them and those that read it, while also feeding negative thoughts in your own mind.

You can combat this negativity by practicing kindness with your social media peers. Leave personalized comments on their posts. Block or report hate speech you encounter. Stand up for others who are being bullied. Play your part and promote digital kindness.

The Ripple Effect of Kindness

Kindness is like a stone you throw in the ocean. It creates countless ripples and saves many lives. Let's read how selfless compassion and care changed lives.

Sharing Stories of Kindness

Franz Kafka was a renowned author. But it was his empathetic nature and kindness that made him an extraordinary human being. In 1923, he met a little girl who was distraught because she had lost her doll. Kafka was moved by her raw emotions and, the next day, bought her a letter from the lost doll to comfort her.

Sometime later, he even bought her the doll itself. The girl found out years later how Kafka planned the whole story to help her out. She not only learned to deal with loss but also came to understand the ways of the world. This is the power of kindness. Kafka's kindness changed the life of a young little girl and helped her find happiness in letting go (Theule, 2021).

The ripple effect of kindness is a powerful thing. A small act of kindness can have a huge impact on someone's life. That person may then go on to do something kind for someone else, and the chain continues.

Exercises

Exercise 1: Random Acts of Kindness

Performing random acts of kindness cultivates empathy and compassion. It also helps you build meaningful connections.

- Perform small acts of kindness throughout your day.

- Offer compliments, help someone in need, or perform acts of service.

- Practice kindness without expecting anything in return.

Exercise 2: Volunteer Work

Volunteer work has a positive impact on others and contributes to your community.

- Find a local charity or organization that aligns with your values.

- Dedicate your time and skills to support their cause.

- You can engage in volunteer work at your local organizations or community centers.

Exercise 3: Kindness Journaling

Journaling amplifies the positive effects of kindness.

- Set aside time each day to reflect on acts of kindness you have received or witnessed.

- Write about the positive impact these acts had on you or others.

- Cultivate a mindset of gratitude and appreciation for acts of kindness in the world.

Exercise 4: Supportive Relationships

Supportive relationships nurture your soul and foster a sense of belongingness.

- Surround yourself with positive and supportive individuals.

- Nurture your relationships by expressing gratitude, offering encouragement, and being present for others.

- Practice active listening and empathy when interacting with loved ones.

Chapter 10: The Power of Self-Care

Self-care simply refers to "a set of activities you perform in order to sustain overall well-being." These activities help you get rid of anxiety, stress, and depression and promote mental and physical nourishment, fostering your personal growth. It is the act of looking after your own health to enhance the quality of life for yourself.

Self-care is a fundamental aspect of well-being and should be accessible to everyone. There are several misconceptions about it. People often regard self-care as being selfish or it being a luxury. They think of it as a time-consuming task that is a temporary fix only.

But you need to realize that these are mere myths that misdirect you. Self-care is a healing remedy that varies from person to person, and it is something we all need to be practicing.

This chapter will shower light on the importance of self-care and the activities you can indulge in to perform it.

Prioritizing Your Needs

To prioritize yourself and your needs means recognizing what you are lacking and then fulfilling it by taking care of yourself. It involves giving importance to your well-being and personal requirements.

To effectively prioritize your needs, you need to accept their significance in various aspects of your life. By giving your needs an upper hand, you develop a satisfactory growing pattern. Your boundaries are set, and your relationships are improved. You have smooth social networks and build up effectiveness and productivity in yourself.

By constant evaluation of what needs serve you well, you can prioritize them efficiently. In order to learn how to prioritize your needs, these are a few simple steps you should follow:

- Be aware of yourself, likes, and dislikes.

- Make decisions in your favor.

- Be compassionate about yourself.

- Practice self-advocacy.

What Do You Mean by Burnout

Burnout is "a chronic state of exhaustion pertaining to your emotional, mental, and physical health. It is caused by constant stress for a long period of time and by overloading oneself with responsibilities."

Not prioritizing yourself makes you overburden yourself. You may easily become exhausted, irritated, and annoyed. Your rate of productivity decreases, and you may encounter recurring headaches. These are all signs of burnout. It is important to recognize them before you face any serious illness.

Burnout is a clear indication of neglecting self-care and prioritizing others over yourself. Ignorance toward your own care leads you to continuous stress, physical overload, and emotional disturbances. You face mood swings, and your personality traits develop anger and being annoyed very easily.

In order to refrain from adopting all these things, you must indulge yourself in self-care activities from time to time to restart and reboot your mental state.

Physical Self-Care

"Taking proper care of your body and its needs" is *physical self-care*. Providing your body with adequate amounts of nutrition and hydration. Also, exercising and keeping your body in active motion. We all are well aware of the fact that *a healthy body possesses a healthy mind*. So practicing self-care in order to generate a fit and strong body is a must.

Following are some easy steps to promote your physical self-care practices:

- Proper nutrition and hydration: By providing your body with adequate amounts of essential nutrients, minerals, and vitamins, you can ensure its healthy development. And by staying hydrated, you can maintain effective physical functioning.

- Regular exercises: Pertaining to physical activities that promote physical health is one of the best self-care methods to adopt. Also an easy one. You can effectively manage weight, prevent the risk of disease, and remain active throughout your day.

- Balanced diet: Physical self-care involves keeping a check on your daily diet. Try to add healthy items like vegetables, meat, and dairy to your diet. Avoid eating too much fast food. Likewise, drinking fruit juices, milkshakes, and yogurt smoothies instead of caffeine, fizzy drinks, or alcohol is preferred.

- Healthy sleep pattern: Fulfillment of daily dose of sleep with proper sleep hygiene is necessary. Establishing a healthy sleep routine and ensuring the quality of your sleep is a step to promote physical self-care.

- Movement and motion: Making body movements by exercising makes your body habitual of working. Working out and inducement in different postures, either by yoga, helps release pain from your body. It makes you fitter, and you can carry out several tasks efficiently.

By implementing the above remedies, you can provide relaxing and resting periods to your body from time to time. Your body will grow strong and will effectively help you carry out further tasks. If you fail to give comfort to your body, its health and condition will begin to deplete, and it will no longer be able to perform like it used to.

Mental and Emotional Self-Care

Emotional well-being is "the ability to process your emotions and regulate them according to the given situations. It is a state of mind that allows you to foster positive emotions and enhances productive cognitions." Your emotional well-being is a fundamental key that makes you cope with challenges and hindrances in the best possible manner.

Whereas *mental well-being* is "that state of mind that allows you to control your perceptions and your reactions. It boosts your ability to function in the best possible way." Your mental health controls your impulses and generates ideas and creations in your mind.

Strategies for Emotional and Mental Self-Care

"Taking essential measures to promote mental and emotional health" is *self-care*. Performing mindful activities and shifting to positive ways of living will benefit you, and it will raise you mentally and emotionally.

Here are some healthy activities for mental and emotional self-care that you can practice:

- Mindfulness and meditation: Regularly engaging in activities like praying, consolation, and meditation can ensure mental growth. These practices arise mindfulness in you and make you more aware and conscious of your surroundings. Your senses become active, and you develop a vigilant personality trait.

- Self-reflection and expression: Performing self-reflection and self-expressive techniques to add to your mental and emotional growth is a very effective method. It makes you think about yourself and express and share thoughts and beliefs. Hobbies like painting, writing, and journaling can help you clear unnecessary thoughts from your mind.

- Seeking support and acceptance: By reaching out to trusted people around you, like friends or family, to share thoughts, feelings, and emotions, you can deliberately clear what's going on in your mind. Knowing that you have emotional support, you let go of negative emotions and create space for positive ones. This promotes your mental and emotional well-being.

- Self-compassion in reducing stress and anxiety: By being understandable and kind to yourself, you can foster healthy mental and emotional states of mind. Treating yourself with the same kind of compassion and gratitude will ensure beneficial growth in mental and emotional health.

- Being realistic in goal setting: Being realistic and accepting the actual way of things around you is another way to promote mental nourishment. By setting acceptable goals and breaking them into small steps, you can cultivate motivation which adds to your mental and emotional well-being.

- Limiting negative exposure: You can do this by being aware of your surroundings and try not to focus on their negative aspects. Limit exposure to negative content on social media. Try to reduce negative thoughts that lower your self-esteem.

Establishing Boundaries

Boundaries are "those comfort lines that hold limits to anything. These are referred to as guidelines that define your comfort zone and protect your mental, emotional, and social well-being." They show how you interact and are comfortable with others. Boundaries can be physical, mental, emotional, time based and differ widely from person to person.

The significance of setting personal boundaries lies in the fact that your privacy regarding personal space is maintained and that you are valued and respected.

Setting boundaries and limitations allows you to prioritize your comfort. It promotes self-respect and self-establishment and works on maintaining healthy relationships as well. It marks an improvement in overall well-being by reducing the risks of physical burnout and stress.

Methods to Cultivate Healthy Boundaries

By cultivating personal boundaries, you carve a way toward overall personal growth. If you are exploring ways on how to set personal boundaries, here are some options for you:

- identify your limitations

- identify your mental, emotional, material, internal, conversational, physical and time boundaries.

- embrace the power of saying NO, so that you can say YES to the things you want

- communicate your boundaries and feelings with honesty to people around you

- RESPECT not only your own boundaries but those of others as well

What Does Saying "No" Mean?

Every situation bears two faces. The front picture and the back picture. The back picture in setting boundaries is saying "no". Refusing to do something that makes you uncomfortable or upsets you is very important in setting and maintaining your private space. It means to deny actions that disturb your mental peace and set you in unrest.

The power of saying "no" engages you in healthy communication and preserves your mental peace. It is an assertive technique to value your personal space and protect your time, energy, and well-being. By saying "no," you can escape hefty situations that overwhelm you and disrupt your mental health.

Learning to say "no" is one of the most essential aspects of establishing healthy boundaries and maintaining them.

Self-Care Activities and Rituals

Self-care activities and rituals are "practices that you perform to nourish and nurture your emotional, physical, and mental well-being. These are those activities that reboot and relax your body systems."

These rituals may vary from person to person depending upon individual preferences and priorities. Every person has their own self-care favorites according to their tastes. Some people tend to follow them routinely; others only indulge themselves in them when they feel the need to do so. Various kinds of activities promise self-care and peace to you these days. A few are listed below:

- isolation and meditation

- physical activity like running, jogging, dancing, swimming, etc.

- pampering yourself with a full-body scrub, having a spa day, or treating yourself to a delicious meal

- engaging in hobbies that rejuvenate and relax you. It may be journaling, reading, painting, listening to music, gardening, etc.

These are some of the basic self-care activities that people follow. Other than these, connecting to nature through hiking or road trips can also rejuvenate you.

Furthermore, prioritizing self-relaxation and your desires and practicing gratitude and self-compassion are measures that compensate for self-care in you. You can encourage yourself to find ways and acts that please your mind and add to your mental satisfaction. By creating your own self-care rituals and making schedules and follow-up routines to engage in them, you avoid stress and physical and mental burnout.

Overcoming Barriers to Self-Care

To indulge in a healthy self-care routine, you need to recognize what refrains you from doing so. Recognizing what impairs you to perform self-care activities is crucial because these are obstacles and hindrances in the way of your personal developmental and healthy growth. These are barriers that restrict your healthy progress.

Overcoming these barriers is a challenge in itself that requires time and effort. With good intentions and consistent efforts, you can overcome these obstacles and incorporate self-care into your lifestyle.

Common Barriers to Self-care

By identifying what are the barriers that restrict you from indulging in self-care activities, it will be a lot easier to eradicate them. These are often discouraging thoughts and beliefs that give a negative impression of self-care and generate false misconceptions about it. The nature of these barriers and hindrances may be internal or external, like lack of self-compassion and overload of responsibilities relatively.

Common beliefs and thoughts that work as obstacles to indulging in self-care activities are:

- time constraints and busy schedules

- guilt and self-worthlessness thoughts

- lack of motivation

- fear of judgment and criticism

- prioritizing others over yourself

Strategies to Overcome Barriers

Eradicating the barriers that restrict self-care is very important because they obstruct your mental growth. These barriers play the role of stones in your constructive pathway toward success. That is why it is necessary to recognize and deal with them beforehand. Some of the simple remedies that can help you eliminate them are:

- learning to prioritize your needs and desires

- challenging limiting beliefs

- letting go of perfectionism

- setting boundaries and practicing time management

- adaptability and accountability

So, by being aware of habits that please your mind and body and recognizing what obstructs them, you can work on creating a healthy self-care routine for yourself. No one but you knows better what suits you and how to cultivate a sustainable self-care routine for yourself.

Celebrating Progress and Success

Self-care is vulnerable to success and progress. Recovering from obstacles and milestones is a long-term motivation and exhibits an emotion of well-doing in you. It creates a sense of self-appreciation and self-confidence. Positive remarks when you achieve your desired goals do the job.

When you work day and night to turn your ambitions into hard-earned achievements, a sense of self-appreciation develops in you ultimately. Your mind and body want a break from hard work and signal you to treat yourself with compassion and light-heartedness.

In this setting, it is crucial to celebrate success and progress to acknowledge yourself and boost your self-esteem. It helps you to remain motivated and perform better in the future. Maintaining your progress and keeping what you have earned so far is done by celebrating previous achievements.

Here are some simple ways of celebrating success and maintaining it:

- Reward or treat yourself.

- Share it with others.

- Write it down and keep it in front of you to boost motivation.

- Engage in self-appreciation.

- Set new goals.

- Practice self-compassion and thankfulness.

Remember that celebrating your success is not about comparing yourself with others. It pertains to promoting self-appreciation and sharing your unique journey. It is a reflection on your past. How did you achieve a set goal? What difficulties have you faced? How to overcome them?

Celebrating your progress makes you ready for further challenges and builds self-confidence in you. It contributes to further mental growth.

Embracing a Life-Long Self-Care Journey

Continuity in self-care fosters personal growth. Embracing self-care emphasizes the fact that self-care is not a temporary or one-time fix but a long-term one. It signifies the value of self-care to boost your morale and enhance your capabilities. By adapting self-care practices, you learn to value yourself, which is a long-term benefit. It is basically a repetitive remedy that helps you navigate through different phases of life.

By embracing the need for self-care in your life, you will realize that it is not a mere fix but has lifelong after-effects in helping you eliminate negativity and restarting and freshening your mind and body. Caring for your own self depicts that you have the ability to take care of others as well. You become wise and acknowledged by people around you for how well you handle yourself and the matters around you.

All the above-mentioned practices of self-compassion, adaptability, prioritization, and success celebration are ways to embrace self-care as a long-term commitment. By indulging in them and gradually making them a habit, you will be able to visualize the differences self-care brings into your life.

These ways make you agree with the fact that self-care indulgences are not a selfish act but a necessary step to take toward your overall well-being and happiness. Seeing how self-care fosters mental and physical health in a positive way, you will be assured about the life-long favor self-care offers you.

Exercises

Exercise 1: Self-Care Rituals

By making time for activities that bring joy and happiness to you, you can foster your personal development. These activities are bound to relax and rejuvenate you. What you need to do is:

- Identify activities that bring calmness and peace to you.

- Incorporate self-care rituals in your routine according to your likeness.

- Prioritize yourself by realizing your worth. This activity nourishes you with positivity and replenishes your energy, fostering overall well-being.

Exercise 2: Setting Boundaries

By being aware of your comfort levels and limitations, you can establish boundaries that decrease your chances of meeting unlikely situations like fights or quarrels.

To do so:

- Identify areas where you think your personal space is breached.

- Be assertive in communicating and networking your boundaries with others.

- Have respect for other people's boundaries so that they do the same.

Boundary setting enables you to protect your time and energy and promotes overall well-being.

Exercise 3: Celebrating Achievements

By celebrating previous progress that you've made, you make yourself more prone to success in the future. Its key role is to help maintain what you have achieved so far. To celebrate success, you should implicit the following practices:

- Appreciate your achievements and milestones, no matter how small.

- Self-reflect on what you've achieved so far and how far you still have to go.

- Reward yourself for accomplishing set goals.

This exercise promotes success by celebration and encourages you to do better. It plays a role in helping you keep up with what you've achieved so far.

Exercise 4: Self-Reflection and Goal Realignment

By practicing self-reflection, you generate a positive thought process that helps you achieve your desired goals more effectively. Here's how you can align your goals accordingly:

- Take time daily to reflect on yourself and self-inspect.

- Review your goals and see if they are still in alignment with your personal aspirations.

- Make adjustments if needed, or set new goals which depict clarity.

This exercise ensures that the goals you've set for yourself are in alignment with your aspirations and fit your personality well. It will make sure that your goals are parallel to how you evolve.

Conclusion

The journey toward happiness is not a matter of seconds, minutes, or days; rather, it is a long process that demands consistency. In this book, we have explored 10 essential steps of happiness that can transform your lives and bring you closer to a state of fulfillment and joy. Throughout this work, we have delved into the depths of self-discovery, goal-setting, positive mindset, self-care, and various other aspects that contribute to our overall well-being.

By understanding yourselves at a deeper level and defining your authentic self, you can lay the foundation for personal growth and happiness. We also learned to let go of people-pleasing and the limitations imposed by fear and past mistakes. Instead, we embraced change and discovered the power of saying "no" to what doesn't serve us, enabling us to say "yes" to what truly matters.

Setting goals is a fundamental part of your journey as well. Hence, we discovered the importance of having a clear vision and identifying your *why*. We learned that successful people don't leave their happiness and success to chance but rather break down their big plans into smaller, achievable goals. By writing down your dreams and visualizing them, you can create a roadmap toward your desired outcomes.

Affirmations and vision boarding are important tools to shape your subconscious mind and cultivate a positive self-image. By speaking kindly to yourselves and visualizing your desired reality, you get to harness the power of your thoughts to manifest happiness and success.

Mindfulness became a sanctuary in which we discovered the beauty of the present moment. Through self-reflection and cultivating awareness, we gained clarity and peace. By observing your thoughts, emotions, and sensations without judgment, you can access a deeper understanding of yourselves and make conscious choices that align with your well-being.

Also, remember that self-control and lifelong habits are the building blocks of your happiness and success. By developing discipline and self-awareness, you can recognize your triggers and temptations and learn to control them. By practicing delayed gratification, setting boundaries, and implementing daily habits that promote well-being, you can create a solid foundation for a balanced and fulfilling life.

Moreover, prioritizing our health and wellness is a cornerstone of your journey toward happiness. You can recognize the importance of moving your body by breathing fresh air and connecting with nature. Engaging in regular physical activity and nourishing your body with nutritious food become acts of self-love.

Finally, we also explored the transformative power of self-care. By setting boundaries, celebrating your achievements, and implementing the knowledge gained throughout this journey, you can replenish your energy and create a foundation for personal growth and fulfillment.

Understand that self-care is not a luxury but a necessity, and by prioritizing yourself, you can better equip yourself to bring happiness and light into the lives of others. As said by mental health clinician and author of *Be Happy Now*, Deborah Day: Nourishing yourself in a way that helps you blossom in the direction you want to go is attainable, and you are worth the effort."

Now go look in the mirror and give yourself a high five for finishing this book and getting started on your new journey to a happier, healthier life.

Glossary

Accountability: Being answerable for your actions and decisions, taking responsibility for outcomes, and fostering trust and transparency in your governance and conduct.

Affirmations: Positive statements used to reinforce self-belief, cultivate optimism, and foster a constructive mindset for personal development.

Attitude: A person's outlook, feelings, and beliefs toward something, influencing their behavior and responses in various situations.

Boundaries: Personal limits and guidelines that individuals establish to protect their physical, emotional, and mental well-being in relationships and interactions with others.

Burning Out: A state of physical, emotional, and mental exhaustion that results from prolonged and excessive stress.

Compassion: A deep feeling of empathy and concern for the suffering or difficulties of others, leading to a desire to help and alleviate their pain.

Coping Mechanism: Adaptive strategies and behaviors individuals use to manage stress, handle challenges, and maintain emotional well-being.

Decluttering: Letting go of physical and mental clutter to achieve a sense of clarity, order, and improved well-being.

Doubt: A state of uncertainty or lack of conviction about the truth, reliability, or validity of something.

Emotions: Complex and subjective states involving feelings, thoughts, physiological changes, and behavioral responses, influencing human experiences and actions.

Empathy: The ability to understand and share the feelings, emotions, and perspectives of others, showing compassion and support.

Forgiveness: The act of letting go of resentment and granting pardon to someone for their perceived wrongdoing or offense.

Goal: Desired outcome or purpose, driving motivation to achieve something specific within a set timeframe or conditions.

Gratitude: A sincere feeling of appreciation and thankfulness toward people, experiences, or circumstances that bring joy and positivity to life.

Introspection: A self-reflective process of examining one's thoughts, emotions, and actions to gain insight and understanding of oneself.

Irritation: A feeling of annoyance, impatience, or discomfort caused by something that bothers or provokes a person's senses or emotions.

Journaling: The act of writing personal thoughts, experiences, and reflections to promote self-awareness, growth, and emotional well-being.

Kindness: The act of showing compassion, empathy, and goodwill toward others, often through thoughtful and selfless actions.

Meditation: A focused practice promoting mindfulness, relaxation, and self-awareness to achieve mental clarity and emotional balance.

Mindfulness: A state of being fully present, aware, and non-judgmental, cultivating focus, inner peace, and emotional resilience for overall well-being.

Mindful Movement: Engaging in physical activities with conscious awareness, focusing on breath and sensations, promoting mind-body connection and stress reduction.

Mindset: A set of beliefs, attitudes, and perspectives that shape one's approach to life, influencing behavior, decisions, and success.

Moment Awareness: Being fully present in the current moment, attentive and mindful of one's thoughts, feelings, and surroundings.

Obstacle: A barrier or challenge hindering progress, requiring effort or strategy to overcome and achieve the desired goals.

Optimism: A positive outlook and belief that favorable outcomes are possible, even in challenging situations, fostering hope and resilience.

People Pleaser: Someone who seeks constant approval and prioritizes others' happiness over their own, often at their expense.

Positive Mindset: An optimistic outlook that focuses on possibilities, resilience, and growth, fostering well-being and success.

Positive Influence: The beneficial impact or effect one person, idea, or action has on another, inspiring growth, improvement, or positivity.

Resilience: The ability to adapt, recover, and thrive despite facing challenges, stress, or adversity.

Self-Care: The practice of prioritizing one's well-being, both physically and emotionally, through intentional actions that promote self-nourishment, relaxation, and rejuvenation.

Self-Control: The ability to regulate one's emotions, impulses, and behaviors to achieve long-term goals and make wise decisions.

Self-Reflection: The contemplation and examination of thoughts, emotions, and actions for personal growth and understanding.

Self-Talk: The internal dialogue or thoughts one has with themselves, influencing emotions, perceptions, and self-beliefs.

SMART Criteria: It is an acronym based on Specific, Measurable, Achievable, Relevant, and Time-bound—guidelines for setting effective goals.

Temptations: Desires or urges to engage in pleasurable or impulsive actions, often conflicting with long-term goals or values.

Vision: A clear, inspiring mental picture of future goals, guiding actions and decisions with purpose and determination.

Wellness: An overall state of physical, mental, and emotional well-being, achieved through balanced lifestyle choices and self-care practices.

References

Achieve Health Goals With Optimism/Positive Thinking. (2013, October 16). WebMD.

An, H.-Y., Chen, W., Wang, C.-W., Yang, H.-F., Huang, W.-T., & Fan, S.-Y. (2020). The Relationships between Physical Activity and Life Satisfaction and Happiness among Young, Middle-Aged, and Older Adults. *International Journal of Environmental Research and Public Health, 17*(13), 4817. https://doi.org/10.3390/ijerph17134817

C. R. Legein-Vandenhoeck, M. (n.d.). *Manu, Your Life Coach & Healer Partner | ABOUT MANU Author of 7 Seals.* In Me I Trust: Life Coaching & Healing. Retrieved July 16, 2023, from https://www.life-coach-healer.be/en/about-manu

Crego, A., Yela, J. R., Gómez-Martínez, M. Á., Riesco-Matías, P., & Petisco-Rodríguez, C. (2021). Relationships between Mindfulness, Purpose in Life, Happiness, Anxiety, and Depression: Testing a Mediation Model in a Sample of Women. *International Journal of Environmental Research and Public Health*, *18*(3). https://doi.org/10.3390/ijerph18030925

E. Sheeran, M., Baird, P., Webb, M., & Harris, T. L. (2016). *APA PsycNet*. https://psycnet.apa.org/doiLanding?doi=10.1037%2Fxge0000185

Franklin, B., Lemay, L., & Zall, P. M. (1981). *The autobiography of Benjamin Franklin: a genetic text*. University Of Tennessee Press.

Glasnapp, J. (2019, October 7). *Council Post: How*

To Practice Self-Affirmations And Reap The Rewards. Forbes. https://www.forbes.com/sites/forbescoache scouncil/2019/10/07/how-to-practice-self-affirmations-and-reap-the-rewards/?sh=632591331a51

Goldman, R., & Young, A. (2022, November 4). *Affirmations: What They Are and How to Use Them*. Everyday Health. https://www.everydayhealth.com/emotional -health/what-are-affirmations/

Harvard Health. (2019, March 21). *Benefits of Mindfulness*. HelpGuide.org. https://www.helpguide.org/harvard/benefit s-of-mindfulness.htm

Reistad-Long, S. (2013). Positive Thinking Sets You Up for Success. WebMD.

https://www.webmd.com/balance/features/
power-positive-thinking

Happiness Quotes (17612 quotes). (n.d.).
Goodreads. Retrieved July 15, 2023, from
https://www.goodreads.com/quotes/tag/ha
ppiness?page=2

Johns Hopkins Medicine. (2019). *The Power of
Positive Thinking.* Johns Hopkins Medicine
Health Library.
https://www.hopkinsmedicine.org/health/w
ellness-and-prevention/the-power-of-
positive-thinking

Langshur, E., & Klemp, N. (2021, May 17). *How
Present-Moment Awareness Can Make Life
More Meaningful.* Mindful.
https://www.mindful.org/how-present-
moment-awareness-can-make-life-more-

meaningful/

Lee, H. (1960). *To Kill A Mockingbird*. Chelsea House Publishers.

McLeod, S. (2023, June 30). *Maslow's Hierarchy of Needs*. Simply Psychology. https://www.simplypsychology.org/maslow.html

M. McMahon, D. (2004). *The history of happiness, 400 B.C. - A.D. 1780*. American Academy of Arts & Sciences. https://www.amacad.org/publication/history-happiness-400-bc-ad-1780

Mandela, N. (2013). *Long walk to freedom: the autobiography of Nelson Mandela*. Little, Brown.

Metcalf, M. (n.d.). *The power of visualization techniques to achieve your goals*.

Mindfulness. (2022). Apa.org.

https://www.apa.org/topics/m

indfulness

Mayo Clinic Staff. (2020, September 15). *Mindfulness exercises.* Mayo Clinic. https://www.mayoclinic.org/healthy-lifestyle/consumer-health/in-depth/mindfulness-exercises/art-20046356

Mao, H.-Y., Hsieh, A.-T., & Chen, C.-Y. (2012). The relationship between workplace friendship and perceived job significance. *Journal of Management & Organization*, 595–627. https://doi.org/10.5172/jmo.2012.595

Payne, J. E., Chambers, R., & Liknaitzky, P. (2021). Combining Psychedelic and Mindfulness Interventions: Synergies to Inform Clinical Practice. *ACS Pharmacology &*

Translational Science, 4(2), 416–423.

https://doi.org/10.1021/acsptsci.1c00034

Physical Activity Quotes (25 quotes). (n.d.). Goodreads. Retrieved July 15, 2023, from https://www.goodreads.com/quotes/tag?utf 8=%E2%9C%93&id=physical+activity

Robbins, T. (n.d.). *What is Positive Thinking? 5 Ways to Use the Power of Positive Thinking.* Tonyrobbins.com.

https://www.tonyrobbins.com/positive-

thinking/

Reynolds, G. (2016, November 16). How Exercise Might Keep Depression at Bay. *The New York Times.* https://www.nytimes.com/2016/11/16/well/ move/how-exercise-might-keep-depression-at-bay.html

Rowland, L., & Curry, O. S. (2018). A range of

kindness activities boost happiness. *The*

Journal of Social Psychology, 159(3), 340–

343.

https://doi.org/10.1080/00224545.2018.146

946

Self-control. (n.d.). APA Dictionary of Psychology.

https://dictionary.apa.org/self-control

Steensen Nielsen, K. (2020, March 2). *People with*

More Self-control are Less Stressed Out.

SPSP. https://spsp.org/news-

center/character-context-blog/people-more-

self-control-are-less-stressed-

out#:~:text=People%20who%20have%20gre

ater%20self

sy@dmin. (2022, January 18). *The Power of No:*

Why Saying "No" is Important. Synergy

Health Programs.

https://synergyhealthprograms.com/why-saying-no-is-important/

Taylor, M. (2022, June 8). *What to Know About Positive Affirmations.* WebMD. https://www.webmd.com/balance/what-to-know-positive-affirmations

The Science Behind Positive Affirmations. (2021, February 4). Third Space. https://www.thirdspace.london/this-space/2021/02/the-science-behind-positive-affirmations/#:~:text=It%20fires%20up%20your%20neural

Theule, L. (2021). *Kafka and the Doll.* Penguin.

What Is Mindfulness? (n.d.). Taking Charge of Your Health & Wellbeing. https://www.takingcharge.csh.umn.edu/wha

t-mindfulness

Yeonmi Park. (2016). *In Order To Live*. Penguin Books Ltd.

Printed in Great Britain
by Amazon

44576345R00145